The Management and Employee Development Review

Competitive Advantage through Transformative Teamwork and Evolved Mindsets

T0383884

The Management and Employee Development Review

Competitive Advantage through Transformative Teamwork and Evolved Mindsets

Kelly Graves

CRC Press
Taylor & Francis Group
Boca Raton London New York

CRC Press is an imprint of the
Taylor & Francis Group, an **informa** business
A PRODUCTIVITY PRESS BOOK

CRC Press
Taylor & Francis Group
6000 Broken Sound Parkway NW, Suite 300
Boca Raton, FL 33487-2742

© 2017 by Kelly Graves
CRC Press is an imprint of Taylor & Francis Group, an Informa business

No claim to original U.S. Government works

Printed on acid-free paper

International Standard Book Number-13: 978-1-138-21620-4 (Paperback)
International Standard Book Number-13: 978-1-138-40000-9 (eBook)

Visit the Taylor & Francis Web site at
http://www.taylorandfrancis.com

and the CRC Press Web site at
http://www.crcpress.com

I would like to dedicate this book to:

My mom Rosie for loving me unconditionally

My daughter Sophia for teaching me how to love unconditionally

And to Katarina: Love and truth transcend time and space

Contents

SECTION III DEPARTMENT DEVELOPMENT LEADS TO COMPANY SUCCESS

Preface

The Search for Meaning

To understand human nature, I believe we must start with the core issue of survival. What makes people want to endure, to survive, and ultimately to live? No better research has ever been done on this topic than by Viktor Frankl, a psychiatrist who lost his wife and children to the gas chambers of Auschwitz and Dachau. Like many European Jews, Frankl experienced firsthand the daily atrocities of life in the Nazi concentration camps during World War II. His research, which he presented in his landmark 1946 book, *Man's Search for Meaning*, was compiled on scavenged scraps of paper. These personal reports, filled with Frankl's keen observations, provide invaluable data about the essence of the human soul. Invaluable, but not priceless—because we understand now the full, intolerable price of that knowledge. We must, therefore, cherish Frankl's horrifying yet ultimately redeeming glimpse into the meaning of life. He and many others in the camps knew not what it was like to survive each day, but only how to survive each breath, not knowing if they would live to take another.

You may be asking yourself, "What does this have to do with business?" This has everything to do with business because the foundation of any company is not its facilities, its inventory, its lines of credit, or even its coveted research and intellectual capital. The building blocks of any business are its people—the organization's greatest asset. How do people think, what drives them, what hurts them, how do groups naturally form and work with or against one another, and what makes them push beyond their limits and follow their inner voice in the face of uncertainty? The answers to these questions are what this book is all about.

Frankl's research is heartbreakingly clear: Those prisoners who gave up on life, who lost all hope for the future, were inevitably the first to die.

"They died less from lack of food or medicine than from lack of hope, lack of something to live for" (Frankl 2006, p. 76). As terrible as it was, Frankl's experience in Auschwitz reinforced what was already one of his key theories: "Life is not primarily a quest for pleasure, as Sigmund Freud believed, or a quest for power, as Alfred Adler taught, but a quest for meaning" (p. x). The greatest task for any person is to find meaning in his or her life. Frankl saw three possible sources for meaning: in work (doing something significant), in love (caring for another person), and in courage during difficult times. Suffering in and of itself is meaningless; "we give our suffering meaning by the way in which we respond to it" (Kim 2012).

The most enduring insight Frankl teaches is that forces beyond one's control "can take away everything you possess except one thing, your freedom to choose how you will respond to the situation" (p. x). One cannot control what happens in his or her life, but one can always control what one feels about the circumstances into which one is placed.

In one memorable passage, Frankl encompasses the sheer power of hope and what happens when people lose it:

> "The death rate in the week between Christmas, 1944, and New Year's, 1945, increased in camp beyond all previous experience. The explanation for this increase did not lie in the harder working conditions or the deterioration of the food supplies or a change in the weather or new epidemics. It was simply that the majority of the prisoners had lived with the naïve hope that they would be home again by Christmas. As the time grew near and there was no encouraging news, the prisoners lost courage and disappointment overcame them. This had a dangerous influence on their powers of resistance and a great number of them died." (Frankl 2006, p.76)

As you are digesting those words, I want to give you some more. Philosopher Friedrich Nietzsche once wrote, "He who has a why to live for can bear with almost any how." If you get nothing else from reading this book, learn this: As a leader of people, it is imperative above all else to provide that "why" to your team: to give them something to believe in which is bigger than themselves. Provide them with a clear destination, and make sure that they understand that this goal is paramount for the success of the organization and the department, but more importantly, how it directly impacts their lives. If you honestly and genuinely involve and touch your people with these concepts and teach them how to own them, you will not only be revered as a good leader of men and women, but you will be a feared competitor within your industry.

The central objective of a great leader and manager of people is to touch your employees at their core so they see and believe in your vision as fervently as you. To achieve this higher state, one must climb inside the mind of their employees and tap into their intrinsic motivation.

"Intrinsic motivation is the self-desire to seek out new things and new challenges, to analyze one's capacity, to observe and to gain knowledge. It is driven by an interest or enjoyment in the task itself, and exists within the individual rather than relying on external pressures or a desire for reward" (Ryan and Deci 2000).

Intrinsic motivation is a natural motivational tendency and is a critical element in cognitive, social, and physical development. Employees who are intrinsically motivated are more likely to engage in the task willingly as well as work to improve their skills, which will increase their capabilities. Employees are likely to be intrinsically motivated if they

- Attribute their results to factors under their control, also known as autonomy
- Believe they have the skills to be effective agents in reaching their desired goals, also known as self-efficacy beliefs
- Are interested in mastering a topic, not just in achieving it for some outside force

An example of intrinsic motivation is when an employee becomes an IT professional because he or she wants to learn about how computer users interact with computer networks. The employee has the intrinsic motivation to gain more knowledge. By doing this, the leader/manager creates a whole out of the disparate individuals and creates the power similar to that of an atom bomb, the major difference being that this process works to create rather than destroy.

"At its simplest, an atomic (fission) bomb does one thing very efficiently: it assembles a 'critical mass' of fission fuel fast enough to start a chain reaction. One liberated neutron strikes a uranium nucleus, releasing energy and more neutrons creating a catastrophic chain reaction" (Broad 2004).

A wise leader's fission fuels are locating and then aligning one's inner desires, their meaning of life, their drives, their inner voice, and mixes these together to create the euphoric explosion, which answers the "why they are going on this journey/adventure with you and achieving something significant with their life; something bigger and more important than themselves."

In the following pages, I'll show you how to overcome the natural tendency to use fear and replace it with psychological techniques that will better align manager and employee work and life goals.

Acknowledgments

Mike Richman for believing in my work and helping me edit this material. Kyle Pugh for doing the wonderful graphics.

Author

Kelly Graves, CEO, Internal Business Solutions Inc., has helped individuals and organizations overcome their most daunting challenges and succeed for nearly two decades. During that time, he has been a key-note speaker at conferences and puts on numerous workshops as well. Graves earned a bachelor's in business and a master's in psychology. Graves has consulted with corporations such as Build.com in Chico, Strachan Apiaries, Yuba College and Valley Truck and Tractor in Yuba City, KPMG in the Dutch Caribbean, Caterpillar in North Carolina, and Wells Fargo in San Diego, as well as many family-owned businesses in need of unique family, transition, and leadership services. Graves wrote a biweekly column for the Chico *Enterprise-Record* called "Work Place" and is a regular contributor for *American Business Journals*, *Sacramento Business Journal*, *Quality Digest Magazine*, and *CEO Magazine*.

To sign up for Graves' newsletter, please visit www.InternalBusinessSolutions.com

If you would like to contact Graves directly, please reach out.

Contact Information
Email: Kelly@InternalBusinessSolutions.com
Website: www.InternalBusinessSolutions.com

THE CURRENT ANTIQUATED MANAGEMENT MODEL

Chapter 1

The Destructive Power of Power

Any man can withstand adversity; if you want to test his character, give him power.

Abraham Lincoln

The Capos

To fully understand how to lead proactively, we must first gain a deeper understanding of the darker side of human nature by revisiting life behind the barbed wire of the concentration camps. A "capo" was a prisoner in a Nazi concentration camp who was assigned by the SS guards to supervise forced labor or carry out administrative tasks in the camp. Also called prisoner self-administration, the capos system minimized costs by allowing camps to function with fewer SS personnel. The system was designed to turn victim against victim, as the prisoner functionaries were pitted against their fellow prisoners in order to maintain the favor of their SS guards. If they were derelict, they would be returned to the status of ordinary prisoners and be subject to other capos. Many prisoner functionaries were recruited from the ranks for their brutality toward other prisoners. This brutality was tolerated by the SS and was an integral part of the camp system.

Capos were spared physical abuse and hard labor, provided they performed their duties to the satisfaction of the SS guards. They also had access to certain privileges, such as civilian clothes and a private room. Capos are made, not born, and they walk among most of us every day at work. Many capos who work in today's organizations do not realize how they impact those around them or they justify it as "getting the job done." Next is a story about a great guy who would act as a capo might when he thought the situation warranted it.

Stan was a very experienced VP for a prominent employer I will call BCO, which employed around 1700 employees. I had consulted in various departments of BCO for around six months when the CEO asked me to work with and assess Stan, his managers, and department. I knew Stan from being around the organization, and we had attended meetings together and what I knew of Stan was that he was a great guy. What I did not know at the time was how his employees felt about him. As I started to do my regular rounds of gathering confidential information, I began to hear stories of Stan that didn't fit the person whom I had known and spent time with. Many of his managers and employees told me stories of a tyrant who demanded perfection and would yell at people and get visibly angry when deadlines were not met. The stories all followed a similar theme, and as time went on, I could tell that the stories had a very high probability of being true. You see, Stan worked for a very friendly CEO named Phil, who demanded perfection from his VPs and would not accept mistakes, or at least that is how Stan interpreted Phil's messages to him. So, in turn, when Stan spoke with his employees he was very demanding to the point of being abusive.

I started shadowing Stan, and although I am sure he toned down his directness, frustration, and anger, I could understand what the employees were talking about. Stan was harsh because that is what he thought was needed to "get the job done." It was not personal; it was a management technique that he thought worked for him when push came to shove. After all, that was how he perceived his boss was treating him. I say perceived because a negative perception is a reality, even if it is not intended to be harmful and hurtful.

I spoke with Stan about his behaviors and sure enough he knew he was harsh and at times bordering on abusive, but that is what the CEO expected of him: results. We spoke of many techniques Stan could use to get things accomplished through others without being loud, aggressive, demanding, and abusive, but first, we had to level the playing field and help Stan's employees speak up and explain their hurts in a safe environment. I had individual employees meet with Stan and me and share their feelings with him. Some were very straightforward about the emotional pain Stan had caused them, while others were more reluctant to speak up. Stan's job was to sit and listen while his employees talked about how they interpreted his behaviors over the previous four years. Stan was astonished that his employees viewed him the way they did because Stan saw himself as a friendly manager, which he was, but when challenges became seemingly insurmountable as they often did, he switched management styles and his abusive self emerged; Jekyll and Hyde.

Luckily Stan was coachable and over time most of the hurts were healed through listening on Stan's part, listening on the employees' part, and more honest communication between Stan and all his staff. We discussed his pressures, their pressures, and what they could all do to work as a team to achieve the demanding needs of the internal and external customers. As time went by everyone became more trustful of one another, fixed misunderstandings quicker by speaking up in a respectful way and learning new management and communication techniques, which I will explain in detail throughout this book. The main thing to learn at this point is when pain is thrust upon another, that victim must have a chance to level the emotional playing field in a respectful and meaningful way: "save face" or redeem themselves. Then and only then can the participants move forward and work on their individual professional development.

The Stanford Prison Experiment

The Stanford Prison Experiment was designed to investigate how "easily people would conform to the roles of guard and prisoner in a role-playing exercise that simulated prison life" (McLeod 2016).

In 1973 Philip Zimbardo, PhD, "was interested in finding out whether the brutality reported among guards in American prisons was due to the sadistic personalities of the guards or had more to do with the prison environment." In other words, is the experiment a lesson about how everyday people (and groups consisting of ordinary people), when given too much power, can become sadistic tyrants? While others such as Konnikova (2015) claim, "Casts doubt on that conclusion arguing that the real lesson is the power of institutions to shape behavior, and how people are shaped by those preexisting expectations." In other words, it is the psyche within the individual or the unhealthy environment that creates the managerial capos.

Since the Stanford Prison Experiment, we've learned a lot about the psychology of power. Here's something we've found: power is not inherently good or evil.

Yes, it is true that power fundamentally alters perception. As Adam Galinsky and colleagues put it, "powerful people roam in a very different psychological space than those without power. Power increases confidence, optimism, risk-taking, sensitivity to internal thoughts and feelings, goal-directed behavior and cognition, and creativity. But these are not necessarily bad outcomes. Put to good use, power can have an incredibly positive effect on people. There are so many compassionate teachers, bosses, politicians, humanitarians, and others who wield power, who genuinely want to make the world a better place" (Galinsky 2008).

> "I think a really important point here is that power amplifies the person. It gives already existing personality dispositions and tendencies a louder voice and increases the chances that these tendencies will be given fuller expression. Thus, we must consider interactions between the person and the situation." As Galinsky and colleagues point out, the situation loses its suffocating hold over the thoughts and behavior of the powerful… "and they are left with their opinions, beliefs, attitudes, and personalities to drive their behavior." (Galinsky 2008)

So, both Maria Konnikova and Adam Galinsky are correct. The person can negatively impact his or her environment and the environment can adversely affect the individual. Therefore, we must learn to rise above our automatic impulses and learn how to lead better and manage people. The line between being an active manager and a tyrant can be fragile, and the closer one gets to that line the more blurred it can become.

In my experience, every organization only has about 5% of the employees and managers whom I consider real manipulators. Most people in management and quasi-management roles have every intention of being fair but don't possess the managerial tools to be effective. Now let me explain that many manager trainees, managers, and even experienced executives have read management books, attended workshops, and maybe even been coached by various professionals, but that does not mean they possess the skills to a degree that they can implement them effectively. They know how to answer a true and false test accurately, they may even know how to list the ten ways to be an active manager, but their automatic responses derived over the course of their life often hijacks their brain, and the material is dumped because their frustration takes over or the skills taught were achieved through intellectual means and not behaviorally encoded. In other words, some people know on an intellectual level the answers to the test but cannot for the life of them apply those learned skills. Let me share another story of a brilliant man who knew all the answers to the test and could even write the test but couldn't manage people well enough to save his job.

I had been consulting with an organization for around ten months when the owner decided she wanted to take the organization to a national level. She had met a man years earlier who was COO of a national travel trailer manufacturer. He was polished and assured her that he could take her company national. I was initially apprehensive but acquiesced to the owner's wishes, since she knew the man and had every confidence in him. He and I never met before his moving to the area and arrival the first week on the job. About six weeks had gone by when the owner mentioned to me some misgivings about his style, which tended to lean toward the harsh side whereas hers had been more lenient. I told her that maybe this was good since they would find a happy medium between their two styles and both would benefit from the cross-pollination of styles.

Kurt was to provide a workshop to all the employees about how to communicate and discuss the finer points of Emotional Intelligence or EI. As I watched and listened to him number and explain the multiple points to this excellent process, I was awestruck by the grasp of his knowledge regarding this topic. However, about two hours later, the owner and I saw and heard him "dress-down" an employee in an incredibly demoralizing manner: entirely contrary to what he had just taught. My heart sank immediately because I knew that although he was intellectually superior in his knowledge of communication and EI, his abilities to apply the behavior necessary to leverage the knowledge was severely lacking. In essence, he knew what to do but could not use that knowledge in a meaningful way. The owner and I tried to work with him to bridge this gap, but he thought of himself as superior and would not listen. Eight weeks later he was terminated. This was one of the most heartbreaking examples I have ever witnessed where a person knew all the right answers to the test but couldn't apply them to save himself. On the one hand, it was a great loss to the organization, but on the other, it was a huge blessing we discovered his weaknesses early so we could draw a line in the sand, decide, and move forward in a direction that was overall best for the organization.

Why Management Uses Fear and Punishment

Managers who rule through rigid control, negativity, and a climate of anxiety and fear do so because they do not trust that things will get done any other way. This tactic usually ends up backfiring, however, because fearful employees will not take risks, bring up new ideas, or be honest about problems. Moreover, very few great people with options want to work for a fear-based manager, so over time these managers have trouble attracting capable workers.

In her book *Freedom from Fear*, Nobel Peace Prize winner Aung San Suu Kyi wrote (1996), "It is not power that corrupts but fear. Fear of losing power corrupts those who wield it and fear of the scourge of power corrupts those who are subject to it."

"Fear will get some results because it sets boundaries and consequences," says Manfred F.R. Kets de Vries (2009), distinguished clinical professor of leadership development and organizational change at INSEAD in France. "But most people who manage by fear eventually fall because no one is able to tell them anything. They live in a fantasy world" (Kets de Vries 2009).

Using punishment as a control tool often fosters an environment of fear in the workplace much as it has in prisons. "One side effect of using punishment inappropriately is that employees become afraid to take risks" (Kets de Vries 2009). This is a major problem for any company, because, without some risk, companies cannot grow and gain competitive advantage.

An employee who works in an environment characterized by using fear and punishment may have problems dealing with pressure, because of the tendency to obsess over potential losses from failure rather than the potential gains from success. In the article, "Fear as a Strategy: Effects and Impacts within the Organization," Appelbaum et al. (1998) identified five main types of fear that prevent employees from taking risks. Four of these fears apply directly to the use of punishment in a workplace.

"The first of these is the fear of failure, which is common in many employees and is even more extensive in employees under a manager practicing fear motivation" (Appelbaum et al. 1998). If an employee works up the courage to try something new and then is punished for the result, this employee is far less likely to experiment in the future. An employee experiencing the fear of failure will usually tend to avoid attention by maintaining the status quo. This employee will let opportunities pass by and instead settle for doing what is easy.

The second fear, the "fear of success," though not thought of in the same light as the fear of failure, has a similar effect. Employees will hold back because success may bring isolation from coworkers. This type of fear, like the fear of failure, inhibits the employee's desire and ability to take appropriate risks.

Third comes the "fear of what others think, which has been a problem for many workers because they do not want to be singled out and targeted because of success or productivity. If an employee is constantly worrying whether others have been offended by his or her success, that employee will tend to try to fit back in the group through the suppression of his or her natural talent. The opinions of others often control this employee's thoughts and even actions." This leads to a lack of creative solutions and an employee who cannot or will not present an opinion.

Finally, the "fear of uncertainty troubles managers and front-line employees alike. If the outcome of the event is not entirely known before-hand, an employee may be reluctant to go through with the plan. This person is not willing to risk the comfort and stability of his or her current situation by taking on more responsibility. Obviously, this lack of deter-mination and fear of risk-taking could be very harmful to the company," especially if it permeates the level of management. People at every level in the hierarchy must feel a semblance of control and by talking about the problems and in some cases embellishing problems creates a semblance of control: at least the ability to control information. As a result, fear is often held firmly in place in large part due to the grapevine keeping it alive through gossip.

PUNISHMENT

"Many people define punishment as something meted out to a person who has committed a crime or other inappropriate behavior" (Manfred F.R. Kets de Vries).

"Applying this definition means that the punisher not only intends to end the behavior but also seeks retribution and hurt to the wrongdoer" (Vaden 2004). Punishment can also result in adverse side effects back toward the manager and organization including anger, aggression, and passive-aggressive sabotage.

Fear Creates Short-Term Action but Destroys Long-Term Motivation

It is six a.m., and I am in Atlanta International Airport. People are shuffling around waiting for their plane while others disembark. As I quietly watch businesspeople and parents with families mingle about, I hear a woman screaming into her phone: "Steven where are you? The plane is leaving!"

I could hear her clearly from 100 feet away, and I can feel her pain as it strikes an inner, primal part of me. She rushes over to the boarding agent and pleads with him to hold the plane while her son finds his way back to the gate. Again the woman screams into the phone, the pitch of her voice filled with more terror this time than moments earlier. Again I feel the primal, stabbing pain of her fear. Her son never arrived in time, and the woman had to make a choice to stay and wait for her son or to get onto the plane. Obviously, she waited for her teenage son to arrive and the family missed their flight. I was amazed at how deeply her fear permeated my body and mind. The feelings of fear stayed with me for quite some time, and I thought of her throughout the day as I flew back home to my family.

The problem with using fear as a mover of people is that it does not have boundaries and can inadvertently impact others to which it was unintended. Referring to the airport scenario, I did not know the woman and never came within 100 feet of her and yet I intimately felt the woman's pain and my sense of foreboding remained in my mind, body, and soul for approximately twelve hours. In essence, using fear and punishment with one individual can often go "airborne" like a deadly virus and negatively impact others totally unrelated to the person to which it is directed. Very much like the fission bomb chain reaction discussed earlier. There is a time and place for using punishment but many rules apply, and much after the fact "clean-up" work must be implemented and in the wrong hands, fear and punishment can wreak unknown consequences like an atom bomb in the hands of a novice. In Chapter 5, I will discuss when and how to use punishment, but for now let us turn our attention toward our primal instincts surrounding fear.

Fear is the most primal of all emotions. When faced with a life-threatening event, people and animals alike immediately go into fight-or-flight mode, which causes adrenaline to surge through the body. Instinctively, one of the two choices turns into action. Fear always creates some immediate action, which our forefathers often used to get their employees to work harder or faster. Old adages come to mind, such as, "When I tell you to jump, all I want to hear back from you is 'how high?'" Alternatively, "If you cannot get it done quicker, there are five guys waiting to take your job who can."

Then there was the carrot-and-stick approach. The stick (and accompanying string) was used to hold a carrot in front of the animal to encourage it to run faster or work harder; if the carrot did not work, then the stick was used to beat the poor beast to get it moving. Applied to a human being, nothing will get a person to move more quickly than fear, as these examples will attest: a person yelling fire; fear of failure; fear of losing one's job; or fear of disappointing an esteemed authority figure. Some people say fear is the greatest of all motivators, but nothing could be further from the truth. Fear creates immediate action and movement but in no way is it a motivator. "The term motivation refers to factors that activate, direct, and sustain goal-directed behavior... Motives are the 'whys' of behavior—the needs or wants that drive behavior and explain what we do. We do not actually observe a motive; rather, we infer that one exists based on the behavior we observe" (Cherry 2016). In other words, motivation comes from within an individual and stays long after the manager has retreated into his office. Think of the old oxymoron, "The beatings will continue until attitudes improve." Fear often backfires because it can also paralyze—the classic deer-in-the-headlights syndrome.

When management uses fear, it destroys motivation and often creates in the employee a sense of resentment, resistance, anger or revenge. As paradoxical as it sounds, employees must use these internal mechanisms to defend themselves against the pain of their "core hurts" caused during childhood.

Symptomatic anger often covers up the pain of these emotional wounds from long ago. "These key distressful emotions include feeling ignored, unimportant, accused, guilty, untrustworthy, devalued, rejected, powerless or unlovable—or even unfit for human contact. Self-esteem is endangered— whether through criticism, dismissal or any other outside stimuli that feels invalidating and so revives old self-doubts. If, however, deep down, we still feel bad about who we are, our deficient sense of self simply won't be able to withstand such external threats" (Seltzer 2008).

The Management Philosophy of "Tom the Tyrant" (aka "Yell at a Man First Thing in the Morning and He Works Hard for You the Rest of the Day")

I was raised in a small town where opportunities were limited and jobs were scarce for the kind of uneducated young man that I was in those days. One winter I was lucky enough to secure a job with a local contractor named Tom. I did not care for construction work, but there weren't any other options, so I took what I could get.

It was hard and dirty work, but I was eager and started off working with enthusiasm and determination to do the best that I could. I wanted to prove that I was tough enough to keep up with the physicality of the job. Each day Tom would yell at me for not carrying enough 2 × 4s at a time or not running fast enough between point A and point B. At first, I thought this was normal and that my learning curve was steep due to my inexperience. I was determined to prove to Tom that I could be a successful laborer. No matter what I did, however, he would yell at me (and others) every day before lunch time.

I needed this job and was willing to do anything required to keep it. I had succeeded at other challenges up to that point in my life and knew it was only a matter of time before Tom would notice my improvement and back off on the yelling. I remained confident for the first two or three months, but as time wore on my enthusiasm turned into anger and then hatred for this man who treated me and others so abusively. I started to resent him and made more mistakes when he was around because my mind was on not getting yelled at rather than the task at hand. This only made the yelling more frequent, and my enthusiasm waned even further.

After a few months of this abuse, I asked his brother why Tom yelled so much at me and others. His answer was quick and to the point. He told me that Tom believed that if he yelled at a man first thing every day, the man would be jumpy the rest of the day and scared for his job, and he would work harder to keep it.

After that conversation I quit working so hard because I realized that it did not matter what I did—the abuse was going to continue regardless. I shut myself off from Tom and became reclusive and resentful. When he was not around, I slowed down. If something was not done right, I did not care because he did not care anything for me. I felt bad about myself. My weekends were wrought with fear of the impending Monday morning that would signal five days of abuse and torture. However, I ended up staying for a year because I lived in a small town with limited options. I hated every minute of it and I swore that once gone I would never allow anyone to treat me with such disdain ever again.

Afterward, I returned to college and anytime I felt like quitting I used Tom as a reminder of what waited for me without an education and the leverage it provided. To this day I hate him and what he stood for. Perhaps my time with Tom played a small part in the path I took to improve working conditions for those who had become prisoners like I was, but didn't have the options to leave as I did.

The Unspoken Rules of Communication

We all learn early in life that communication between people has an unspoken set of rules. If someone is talking to you, you pay attention; if someone gives you something, you say, "Thank you"; if someone insults you, you defend yourself in one manner or another. In essence, we all learn that human interaction is reciprocal. When we consider the manager–employee relationship, this point becomes even clearer. Employees prefer a manager who makes them feel as if they can solve their problems, which will help them and coach them but not tell them what to do or do it for them. A manager who disparages his or her employees or displays overt superiority will cause that employee to lose "face." That manager may get short-term results but will be resented by the employees, and will end up with a weaker team.

When an employee loses face in the relationship, not only does that person feel embarrassed, humiliated, and vengeful, but also the manager who caused this result is thereby proven unreliable. Such an unpredictable manager will be ostracized and isolated from his or her employees. In other words, the workers will go "underground" or triangulate among themselves. They will speak poorly of the manager in an attempt to regain their sense of self and prove their worthiness within the group. It is the manager who has broken the code of communication conduct and will ultimately be subject to humiliation through the team's failure to achieve its goals. These behaviors may not be spoken or even understood on the conscious level, but will, in any event, be carried out. In fact, they must be conducted for the individuals involved to maintain any semblance of control over their lives (Figure 1.1).

TRIANGULATION

The concept of triangulation in relationships was originally introduced by Dr. Murray Bowen (1971), who observed that sometimes when people in relationships came across an area of conflict, they avoid dealing directly with the person with whom they are in conflict (and thus the conflict itself) by discussing it with another person who would be more likely to agree with their point of view. This reduces inner tension.

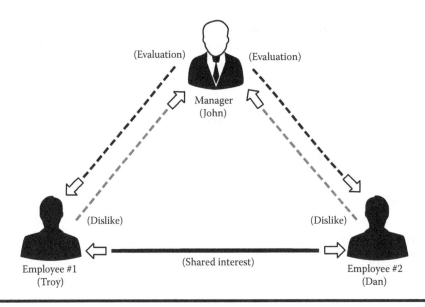

Figure 1.1   Triangulation.

For example, say that Troy is harshly reprimanded by John, who is his direct supervisor. Troy fears losing his job so he must remain quiet and agree with the criticism, whether John's statements are true or not. This causes Troy to feel devalued and powerless and as a result vulnerable. When Troy is released from John's reprimand, he becomes angry because anger provides Troy a semblance of control over his life, and anger feels much better than vulnerability. Troy feels victimized by John, so he seeks out Dan, whom he knows also dislikes John and his management style. When Troy tells Dan about the reprimand they both slam John and his incompetent management style, thus removing some of Troy's initial feelings of powerlessness and again providing him with a semblance of control. Troy justifies this by saying to himself it was not his fault that he made a mistake; it was John's fault for not training and coaching him properly.

What Causes Office Politics to Trump Company Profits

"Office politics" are the strategies that people play to gain an advantage, either personally or for a cause that they support. Both individuals and groups may engage in office politics, which can be highly destructive as people focus on personal gains at the expense of the organization. "Self-serving political actions can negatively influence social groupings, cooperation, information sharing, and many other organizational functions. I call these systems 'us vs. them' cultures" (Graves 2016a).

An overwhelming majority of organizations have inadvertently created an "us vs. them" (Graves 2016b) culture by turning much of their focus and many of their resources away from serving the customer and instead directing them toward fighting one another and vying for power. Alternatively, they may have given up and are just "doing time." Losses are rarely caused by the economy or stiff competition; they are self-inflicted and mainly caused by infighting and various forms of conflict.

People who work in an "us vs. them" culture do so out of necessity. Their days are often focused on the internal problems of the organization rather than on providing better customer service, product improvement, and increasing revenue. Oddly enough, these people started their careers with the best intentions, but over time, small issues turned into overwhelming conflicts until staff and management were reduced to incessant gossiping and finger-pointing (Figure 1.2).

Example: "I do not care what John wants or needs, I'm doing it my way."

BFMC was a machine shop that made precision aluminum parts for the medical industry. John had been promoted from vice president of operations to CEO and was having difficulty leading the other vice presidents. All of

84% of managers don't know how to accurately measure their team members.

32% of team doesn't know their next move in the company.

48% of new hires leave their job within the first year.

78% of US workers said being recognized motivates them in their jobs.

Higher employee engagement resulted in a 50% reduction in reportable accidents from 18% to 9% over a two-year period. (Babcock Marine Clyde)

72% of US workers are not engaged in their work. Defined as essentially sleep walking throughout their day. (Gallup)

Figure 1.2   Employee engagement statistics.

them had held positions in the company for decades, and each man ran his department as if it were his own business. Even the previous CEO, who had recently retired, had experienced some significant challenges in corralling this headstrong group of executives.

When I was hired by the CEO to work with this organization, everyone got along fairly well, partly because no one told anyone else what to do. It was a leaderless and rudderless ship that had weathered ups and downs and made money most of the time but was allowed to drift along because no one wanted to make waves. Even though BFMC made 5%–6% on average gross sales of $40 million, given their industry, their years within the industry, and their product offerings, they should have been consistently averaging 12%–15% on average gross sales of $60–70 million. During the first executive meeting, it was easy to figure out the three fundamental problems plaguing this leadership team:

1. They did not have a strong leader who would make decisions and hold his or her executives accountable.
2. BFMC did not have clear goals nor did they have a plan on how to get from point A to point B.
3. The worst mistake they were making, however, was in-fighting among themselves more than with the competition.

As a direct result of these issues, the company experienced scrap losses that sometimes reached as much as $75,000/month, or around 40% of particular product runs where the industry average was a paltry 2%–3%. The managers argued about who was causing the scrap losses. The engineers who designed the products blamed the machinists, and the machinists blamed the engineers, and both blamed the substandard material the CEO was having the purchasing department buy from China. What we did to correct this devastating discrepancy will be thoroughly addressed in Chapter 7.

What Employees Need from Their Managers and What Managers Need to Learn to Become Great

Most employees deeply want and need an insightful and vigorous leader. In every intake interview I have ever conducted for nearly two decades, the data are clear: People desire a leader who communicates with them, involves them, and establishes accountabilities for everyone in the organization—especially the leader him- or herself. This successful leader learns to set the example by being kind yet firm, makes the decisions, doesn't get pulled off course by pushy people or groups, provides a unified vision that people buy into, outlines a clear path for employees to follow and supports people, so they are successful. Here is a condensed list I have collected from thousands of employees, and what they wanted their CEOs, owners, and managers to hear but were too afraid to tell them directly. Also, these are exactly what managers need to do to make their companies successful: management (Internal Business Solutions, Inc., n.d.).*

1. Get your employees' opinion. Your employees know their job better than anyone else in the company, they know what the customer wants or doesn't want because they work directly with them, and the customer confides in them. This is a manager's greatest asset; use it. You do not need to hire an expensive assessment company. Take that time and money and have some honest conversations with your frontline employees.
2. Listen to your employees. Listen to them and don't multitask when you do. Respect them, and show them that you value their ideas by implementing some of them or discussing the vision or processes with them. (This will empower employees, unite them, involve them, and help them feel pride in what they are building. Most important, they will buy into what they helped create.)
3. Make the decision. Ultimately you are the leader, and so you must make the final determination. They want to be led by a confident and insightful manager whom they trust to lead them through the difficult times and outsmart the competition so that the organization can win. In essence, they need a leader who they admire and are proud of. When done properly they will follow you into hell and back because they have faith you will protect them from the heat. That also means protecting them from the heat from executives who hand down blame. It is the manager's job to take the hit when something goes wrong and to push your employees out front to take their bow when things go well. When you take the hit for them, this will bind them to you because they will know you got the black eye for them, and this will create unbreakable trust. When you let them take the bow, they know you led them there, and yet you handed over the trophy. That is real leadership, and when

---

* Retrieved from http://www.internalbusinesssolutions.com/tag/management/

you as the manager are backed by people who value you, they will surmount heaven and earth to make sure they please you. Who would not want to please such a selfless leader?

4. Don't waiver with your decision. Employees need a leader who is strong-willed and won't be swayed by an overbearing employee or a group who wants special treatment because they have been there longer and feel entitled. Your decision should be made for what is best for the company—period. Be consistent; they may not always like the decision the manager makes but they can admire the consistency. Moreover, consistency in a manager's behaviors and decisions creates consistency in the employees' communication, processes, performance, and quality. Consistency creates safety since people always know where they stand since the lines on the field do not move; they are etched in stone.

5. Give employees a clear vision. The vision should be created with all of everyone's input but synthesized by the manager and delivered back to the employees in a crystal-clear manner. What will be our company and department vision and destination in twelve months, then six months, then three months, and then what do we have to accomplish in the next thirty days to get us on started and on target? Now this makes it clear what we need to achieve this week. Like going on vacation: what's the destination—snowy mountains or white sandy beaches? Why do we want to go there? What will life be like when we get there? How will this destination improve our lives?

6. Outline a step-by-step road map. To make the journey less ambiguous and scary, provide a very clear step-by-step road map for them to follow so that they can follow and trust you even when it is dark or foggy, and they cannot see. What will we like about this trip and what won't we like about this trip? Remember that your employees' livelihoods are in your hands so tell them up front so it will not be a surprise, and they can plan for the regular ups and downs. Also, if you tell them ahead of time about the usual ups and downs, this will inspire trust in you since you knew ahead of time what would probably happen and how to prepare for it. Are they going by plane and will be there in three hours, or by car and they will drive for three days over mountains and across long boring and hot deserts? Are they going by sailboat and since their livelihoods are in your hands, do you know how to work a compass? Spend a little time with your employees and tell them the big picture and inspire trust, and this will reduce their fear and inspire confidence.

7. Support them along the way. Most employees would know their jobs if they were trained and coached properly. However, they constantly need professional development in how to do them better, more efficiently, or how to approach this new vision from a different perspective so that they can fully believe in it and totally support it, even when they are not 100% sure what they are supporting. Employees want to believe in their manager. All a great manager needs to do is provide them with skills and insights so that they can have pride in themselves, in their company, and in you, their leader.

All company success is built with and through its people; as we work our way through this book, I will show managers how to unite and ignite the spark of something bigger than the individual, something they can believe in as a group. The manager is like a conductor of an orchestra. If he or she lacks the skills, there won't be inspiring music for people to hear, but rather disorganized noise. Just like highly trained music conductors, managers of departments must possess leadership skills and be in tune with every musician and instrument. When the manager possesses these skills, they can take musicians from various disciplines and combine them to create beautiful music. Music that each musician had been searching to make his or her entire life. This is what a great producer of a rock band does, an excellent conductor of a symphony does, and the great manager of a department does. Keep reading and become the great creator you were meant to become.

The Destructive Power of Gossip

"Gossip is what keeps fear alive and aids the condemned in feeling better about themselves." (DeGouveia 2005)

For the most part, office gossips and rumors have come to be accepted as part of most work environments. Technology such as the Internet and email facilitate the quick spreading of undesirable communication. "The nature and intensity of gossip have become more severe. Employees will always communicate facts, events and occurrences around them, but when they cross the line between healthy communication and malicious gossip, individual and organizational damage occurs" (DeGouveia 2005).

For the most part, gossip is a familiar part of everyday life. However, gossip tears at the fabric of individuals, groups, and organizations because it breaks down trust between employees and puts additional strain on values such as openness, transparency, and honesty. Thus, morale, motivation, and interpersonal respect between employees are significantly depressed. I compare gossip to our fission bomb example; it grows geometrically at an alarming rate and can unwittingly impact the bottom line and ultimately kill a business. Radiation-fueled "water-cooler talk works steadily and over time affects morale and productivity, resulting in sick days, resignations and premature job searchers as victims of malicious gossip feel alienated, hurt and embarrassed" (DeGouveia 2005, p. 56–68).

DEFINITIONS OF GOSSIP: PART 1

In my personal interactions with clients over the years, I have heard gossip described in various ways, such as

"Talking behind someone's back."
"You know it is gossip when the minute the person (you were talking about) walks in, and you quickly change the topic to the weather."
"Confidential."
"Sensitive."
"Gossip is everything you would not bring up in the boardroom."
"None of your business."
"Blown out of proportion."
"Spreads like wildfire."
"Creates stress/uneasy working conditions."
"Gossip is mostly wrong."
"Someone usually gets hurt."
"Often has negative consequences."
"Making assumptions/fueling speculation."
"Creates false impressions."
"It is talking about someone's personal life without their consent, and adding your two cents' worth when you do not even know the person."
"Prying."
"Speaking out of turn."
"Hearsay."
"Often exaggerated."
"Unrelated to the crucial functioning of the business (does not affect the employee's work performance, but adversely affects the employee/others)."

DEFINITIONS OF GOSSIP: PART 2

"'Women gossip to become friends while men establish a friendship first and once there is a foundation for trust, they gossip.' From the above, it can be said that women open up more easily than men and are more willing to share information. It was the belief of many participants that female friendships are formed and based on office gossip conversation while men first establish a friendship: speaking about cars, sports and motorbikes. Only once the relationship is established and the men are sure that they can trust each other do they start to share gossip information. It was also mentioned that men and women gossip about different things. Men gossip about a single topic while women can gossip about 'anything and everything'" (DeGouveia 2005).

Summary

Frankl's research is heartbreakingly clear: Those prisoners who gave up on life, who lost all hope for the future, were inevitably the first to die. They died less from lack of food or medicine than from lack of hope, lack of something to live for. As terrible as it was, Frankl's experience in Auschwitz reinforced what was already one of his key theories: "Life is not primarily a quest for pleasure, as Sigmund Freud believed, or a quest for power, as Alfred Adler taught, but a quest for meaning. The greatest task for any person is to find meaning in his or her life." Frankl saw three possible sources for meaning: in work (doing something significant), in love (caring for another person), and in courage during difficult times. Suffering in and of itself is meaningless; we give our suffering meaning by the way in which we respond to it (Frankl 2006, p. 76).

Philosopher Friedrich Nietzsche once wrote, "He who has a why to live for can bear with almost any how." If you get nothing else from reading this book, learn this: As a leader of people, it is imperative above all else to provide that "why" to your team, to give them something to believe in that is bigger than themselves. Provide them with a clear destination, and make sure that they understand that this goal is paramount for the success of the organization and the department, but more importantly, how it directly impacts their lives. If you honestly and genuinely involve and touch your people with these concepts and teach them how to own them, you will not only be revered as a good leader of men and women, but you will be a feared competitor within your industry.

Managers who rule through rigid control, negativity, and a climate of anxiety and fear do so because they do not trust that things will get done any other way. This tactic usually ends up backfiring, however, because fearful employees will not take risks, bring up new ideas, or be honest about problems.

We all learn early in life that communication between people has an unspoken set of rules. If someone is talking to you, you pay attention; if someone gives you something, you say, "Thank you"; if someone insults you, you defend yourself in one manner or another. In essence, we all learn that human interaction is reciprocal. When we consider the manager–employee relationship, this point becomes even clearer. Employees prefer a manager who makes them feel as if they can solve their problems, which will help them and coach them but not tell them what to do or do it for them.

Chapter 2

How Employee Evaluations Are Destructive

One reason why performance appraisal in organizations is emotionally resisted so strongly is that managers know full well they are violating the larger cultural rules and norms when they sit a subordinate down to give him or her "feedback." To put it bluntly, when we tell people what we "really think of them" in an aggressive way, this can be functionally equivalent to social murder. Someone going around and doing this is viewed as unsafe to have around, and, if the behavior persists, we often declare such a person mentally ill and lock him or her up.

Edgar Schein (2010)

THE DEFINITION OF THE TERM "EVALUATION"

The *Merriam-Webster Dictionary* provides three definitions of "evaluation"; all of them compare it with "judgment."

1. To judge something with respect to its worth or significance
2. To judge the value or condition of (someone or something) in a careful and thoughtful way
3. To determine the significance, worth, or condition of something, usually by careful appraisal and study

When one person judges another, the judged person must defend. This establishes an adversarial relationship between the manager and the employee, and the trust-based interaction between these two members is often diminished from this point forward.

The human inclination to judge can create serious motivational, ethical, and legal problems in the workplace. Without a more evolved review process, there is little chance of ensuring that the collaboration and mutual development between the manager and the employee will be functional, accurate, equitable, lawful, and (in a case of a legal suit) defensible.

Annual evaluation systems began as simple ways for managers to counsel employees, set goals, identify strengths and weaknesses, and justify those employees' salaries. The objective was to evaluate an employee's performance relative to established standards.

However, the actual way in which evaluations are conducted in most organizations today reflects a history of inconsistency. As a result, mistakes, biases, and abuses occur, which in turn become the source of potential legal liability for employers.

Some managers and human resource professionals still view employee evaluations as necessary to manage performance and make timely accurate staffing decisions. "Done correctly, evaluations can provide systematic judgments to support salary increases, promotions, transfers, demotions, and terminations. They are a means of assessing and communicating job performance" (Juniata 2011). Performance evaluations provide status to an employee and a forum in which needed changes in behavior, attitude, skills, or job knowledge can be shared. They are also used by managers to train, coach, or counsel the individual as well as to identify and deal with specific performance issues.

Other managers and human resource professionals only view them as a necessary evil, or worse yet, as altogether unnecessary. These differing attitudes among managers and HR professionals are partly the cause of employers having to face more and more legal challenges relating to employee evaluations.

The evaluation process has been linked to material outcomes. If an employee's performance was found to be less than ideal, a cut in pay would often follow. "On the other hand, if that person's performance exceeded expectations, a pay raise was in order. Little consideration, if any, was given to the developmental possibilities of the employee. If it was felt that a cut in pay, or a raise, should provide the only required impetus for an employee to either improve or continue to perform well" (Juniata 2011).

"Sometimes this basic system succeeded in getting the results that were intended; but often, it failed.

"For example, early motivational researchers were aware that different people with roughly equal work abilities could be paid the same amount of money and yet have entirely different levels of motivation and performance" (Juniata 2011).

These observations have been confirmed in many empirical studies. Pay rates were necessary, yes; but they were not the only element that had an effect on employee performance. It was found that other issues, such as morale and self-esteem, also were major influences.

Although most companies have an employee evaluation policy in place, many managers do not follow it. Failure to evaluate employees consistently, however, can be the basis for a lawsuit. Employees who have recently been terminated argue that they never had notice of performance problems or that the problems mentioned had nothing directly to do with them. Thus, the current employee evaluation model is often shrouded in an undercurrent of fear on both sides.

For an example of how this plays out in the real world, consider the case of Justin, a copywriter for a marketing department. He has his annual performance review scheduled for 3 p.m., and all day his anxiety has been rising. He is a good employee who turns in his projects on time and gets along well with his manager, John, yet he feels tense and edgy. Justin tries to relax, but it is nearly impossible because he hates being judged. He always leaves these meetings feeling worse than when he went in. John rarely admonishes Justin directly for any rare mistakes, but neither does he acknowledge Justin's many successes accomplished throughout the year.

Finally, the clock reads 2:55. As Justin starts walking toward John's office, his anxiety peaks into the red zone. "Why do I let this happen to me?" he wonders. "I feel like a kid in school who has been sent to the principal's office. This is crazy! I am a good employee and have been working for John for five years now. I got this!" He hears the words but still his mind will not let go of the worry, and his body will not let go of its anxiety. After all, he, his wife, and two young children rely on this job for their living.

Justin knocks on John's door and hears a muffled, "Come in." As Justin enters, John motions toward the table in the middle of his office as he finishes a call at his desk.

Six to seven minutes later, John comes over and apologizes for running late. This is typical, as John is usually late for meetings and seems stressed out most of the time. John laid the filled out evaluation on the table and starts with question one. Even though Justin knows that John is doing his best to be mindful of what he says and how he says it, his words and mannerisms still come across as, "I am the principal, and you are my student, and I need to reprimand you to make you better... moreover, by the way, this is for your own good."

John reads each question and follows up with some prewritten remarks. These tell Justin that although he is doing a good job, he often falls short and should, therefore, try harder, or perhaps spend some time on the weekends brushing up on some new writing techniques, and edit his copy with more attention to detail. Justin thinks that he does edit everything before he sends it out, but his workload is overwhelming, and John regularly gives him assignments at the last minute, all while expecting perfection. Justin feels that if he had a little more notice, he could create better copy, but does not verbalize this thought. After all, he cannot take the chance of losing this job, so he smiles, bites his lip, and keeps his mouth shut.

After all, Justin has been through this before with John and previous bosses, and he knows how to play the game. Just nod, keep your thoughts to yourself, and don't make waves. Every so often during the evaluation, John asks Justin if he understands everything, and inquires if he has anything to add. Once, a long time ago, Justin took the bait and replied honestly to these questions, only to be told he was wrong. So, Justin has now learned to simply nod in agreement, smile that fake smile, and help to move the evaluation along as quickly as possible so he can get out of there. He knows that nothing ever changes, so there's no need to speak up. Plus, everyone in the department knows that John can be unpredictable, so everyone's plan is always the same—get in and get out as quick as possible and be glad that these evaluations only happen every year or so.

When Justin returns to his desk, his buddy Richard slides over and asks, "How did it go?"

"The same old routine," Justin says. "He talked, I listened, I agreed with everything he said, I gave him my best smile and the pain was over in a record 45 minutes. Thank God I do not have to go through that for another year."

"Did he get into any details about anything?"

"No," Justin replied, with a sad smile. Richard was new and would get to experience it for himself when his first year rolled around in another few months. "He never talks about things in detail. He never offers anything constructive. It is the same every year. He does not tell us how to improve or what he likes, and for us to do more of, he just tells us to work harder or longer and get better."

Richard walks away, discouraged and now worrying about his approaching evaluation. They both get back to work, but in the back of their minds, they wonder if the organization is dysfunctional, or if John is, or if they are.

Why Employees Hate Evaluations: Psychological and Sociological Implications

"W. Edwards Deming maintained that when people get unfair negative evaluations, it can leave them bitter, crushed, bruised, battered, desolate, despondent, dejected, feeling inferior, some even depressed, unfit for work for weeks after receipt of the rating, unable to comprehend why they are inferior" (Pfeffer 1999).

The nine responses listed below are from actual employees who have had trouble understanding the value of the current employee evaluation model (Wendy 2013):

1. Managers do not know their employees.

    "I have worked at many jobs where I would rarely be on the same shifts as my managers. How can a manager assess an employee when he or she cannot directly observe that employee's behaviors and performance? As an employee, I did not have a platform where I could log in every task I did on my shift. It became difficult for me to be open for feedback when my manager apparently did not keep track of my progress. I believe that a manager should be up-to-date with an employee's performance rather than relying on others to evaluate how a worker is performing."

2. Managers are not trained properly.

    "The idea behind employee evaluations is for the manager to have one-on-one discussions with his or her employees to talk about how they did and how they can perform better. Instead, managers are provided with a standardized form saying what they need to ask and how to assess each employee. 'The problem is that a standardized process assumes that every employee is the same.' Managers are not given enough support on how to deal with a broad range of emotional responses. When employee evaluations go wrong, it creates a negative relationship between the manager and the employee. Managers do not know how to follow up with the employees without causing further animosity. In my experience, most employees equate evaluations with punishment."

3. In evaluations, there is a thin line between the person and that person's performance.

"My biggest problem with employee evaluations is that the meeting can turn personal very fast. Managers go off on tangents when they do not know how to conduct a proper employee evaluation. The review starts to evaluate the employees' characteristics and behaviors, instead of the work performance itself. I remember an old manager giving me constructive feedback on my 'grumpiness' during an evaluation. The fact that I was grumpy in the morning once never affected my performance at completing my tasks and delivering results. I would be more open to feedback if she took me aside on the spot and talked to me about my grumpiness, rather than wait for the end of the year to bring it up. It is hard to distinguish whether you are being assessed for the final result you deliver or the effort you put into delivering your performance over the course of the year."

4. The process is time-consuming for managers.

"Managers are left on their own to collect the information needed to conduct employee evaluations. They need to keep track of what each employee has done, how well he or she has performed, and other factors that may affect success or failure. There is a high anxiety level for the managers as they have to figure out how to objectively rate the employees fairly and consistently. Managers see employee evaluations as a burden. Their lack of interest affects employees, as the employee evaluation becomes a formality to get the appropriate information to fill out the necessary forms. Employees get nothing out of the employee evaluation other than a total rating for the year, or maybe some arbitrary goals."

5. Employee evaluations create an atmosphere of high anxiety and stress.

"Many companies conduct an annual employee evaluation with no in-between coaching sessions. Employees walk into the meeting without having any idea of how they've done. They do not receive feedback from their managers throughout the year, and so they have not had any opportunities to improve. Being in the unknown makes employees nervous and very defensive. It is even more demoralizing when the outcome of the employee evaluation is linked to your compensation. People get sensitive when their salaries are being altered at someone else's discretion."

6. Communication during employee evaluations is one way.

   "Every employee evaluation I have had was totally management-driven. I had no say in the ratings of my performance and was not welcome to share any feedback. It was a one-way street where my only role was to accept whatever the manager had decided for me. It was disheartening not to be able to contribute to the discussion. I see the lack of transparency as being vague and hypocritical."

7. Employee evaluations are subjective.

   "Our management used some different rating systems to try to make evaluations more objective. One of them was the Behaviorally Anchored Rating Scale (BARS), which provides an example for each rating. The models are used as a benchmark for managers to decide how to rate their employees, but the scoring was still left to the managers' discretion. Different interpretations of the rating scale and an employee's level of performance made the whole process extremely subjective. Using a rating system creates an illusion of objectivity, but employee motivation decreases when their contributions become quantified in an arbitrary way."

8. The manager's mood can alter the evaluation.

   "Sometimes I would have my evaluation when my manager was having a bad day. This tended to make that person a much more assertive evaluator and more attuned to my mistakes and problems. On the other hand, if I caught the manager in a good mood, I was much more likely to be given a break on certain things, or at least the benefit of the doubt. The manager's frame of mind is beyond my control, and that just adds more frustration and uncertainty to the evaluation process."

9. Hypocrisy.

   "I had a manager who seemed to go out of his way to *not* follow stated company policies and procedures. When your manager does not practice what the organization preaches, the contradiction generates disappointment, distrust, and cynicism. It reduces motivation and discourages behaviors that contribute to vibrant, productive, and healthy work environments."

Reasons for Failures

The ideal employee evaluation process is valid, consistent, objective, job-related, and "evidence-based" (Wolfe 2004, pp. 667–696), i.e., supported by reliable documentation. Unfortunately, employee evaluations frequently fail to meet these essential criteria for several reasons:

■ Managers doing the evaluations are not prepared, serious, and/or honest.
■ Managers often use unclear and ambiguous terms, and/or lack knowledge of performance standards.
■ Managers often encourage short-term performance, diminish teamwork, and create destructive rivalries.
■ Managers "evaluate" employees but do not provide ongoing development or feedback.

Conducting performance evaluations in a timely and thorough manner is one of the most important duties of a successful manager, but few take it seriously enough. The current employee evaluation process has proven to be devastating to organizations. Conventional employee evaluations have been linked to high levels of attrition, low productivity, and significant problems with collaboration. PwC's 17th Annual Global CEO Survey, conducted in 2013, found that 93% of the CEOs surveyed recognized the need to change their talent practices—something their companies were doing wasn't working. Meanwhile, per Korn Ferry Institute leadership development researcher Robert Eichinger, the ability to "grow talent" (Rock 2014) is ranked 67th out of 67 competencies for managers, despite decades of investment in employee development systems. In other words, on average, managers are worse at developing their employees than at anything else they do.

A significant cause of the problem is poor informal feedback processes. In general, employees like to receive feedback because, like anyone else, they want to do well. Feedback helps them do their best, and quality performance feedback on an ongoing basis is the lifeblood of the employee evaluation process. "Research and practice demonstrate a consistent disconnect between employee and manager perspectives about the degree and nature of performance feedback" (Rock 2014). As managers must learn, communication is the building block of trust. Survey results, such as those referenced in the sidebar below, indicate that employees desire more frequent, accurate, and timely feedback than the typical manager provides. Furthermore, the research suggests that a significant number of employees do not believe that their managers have the requisite skills to provide appropriate feedback and development. As a result, employees can be aggravated when feedback sessions are superficial, rushed, or even interrupted. Employees consistently ask for direct feedback, not the sandwich approach that managers try when they attempt to hide the negative feedback in between a couple of slices of general compliments (Figure 2.1).

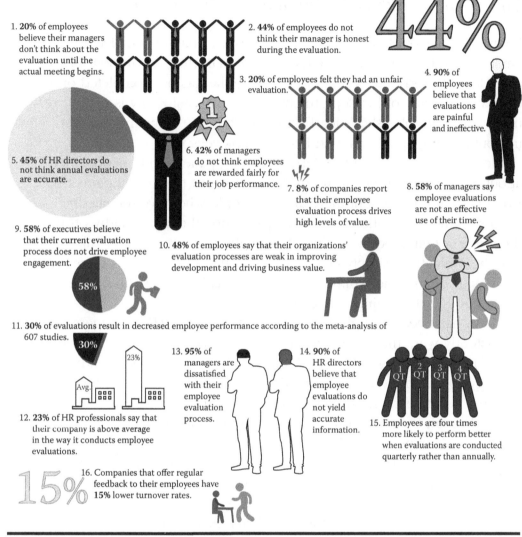

1. **20%** of employees believe their managers don't think about the evaluation until the actual meeting begins.

2. **44%** of employees do not think their manager is honest during the evaluation.

3. **20%** of employees felt they had an unfair evaluation.

4. **90%** of employees believe that evaluations are painful and ineffective.

5. **45%** of HR directors do not think annual evaluations are accurate.

6. **42%** of managers do not think employees are rewarded fairly for their job performance.

7. **8%** of companies report that their employee evaluation process drives high levels of value.

8. **58%** of managers say employee evaluations are not an effective use of their time.

9. **58%** of executives believe that their current evaluation process does not drive employee engagement.

10. **48%** of employees say that their organizations' evaluation processes are weak in improving development and driving business value.

11. **30%** of evaluations result in decreased employee performance according to the meta-analysis of 607 studies.

12. **23%** of HR professionals say that their company is above average in the way it conducts employee evaluations.

13. **95%** of managers are dissatisfied with their employee evaluation process.

14. **90%** of HR directors believe that employee evaluations do not yield accurate information.

15. Employees are four times more likely to perform better when evaluations are conducted quarterly rather than annually.

16. Companies that offer regular feedback to their employees have **15%** lower turnover rates.

Figure 2.1 Information chart. (From Williams, Ray, www.PsychologyToday.com, November 7, accessed October 1, 2016, https://Psychologytoday.com/whyperformance appraisalsdonotimproveperformance, 2012; Barry, Lisa et al. Performance management is broken replace "rank and yank" with coaching and development, accessed October 1, 2016, https://dupress.deloitte.com/dup-us-en/focus/human-capital-trends/2014/hc -trends-2014-performance-management.html, 2014; Knowledge@Wharton, Should Performance Reviews Be Fired?, April 27, accessed October 1, 2016, http://knowledge .wharton.upenn.edu/article/should-performance-reviews-be-fired/, 2011; Mosley, Eric, www.blogs.hbr.com, June 15, accessed October 1, 2016, http://www.blogs.hbr .org/crowdsourceyourperformance, 2012; Dawn, Melissa, www.sap.com, July 11, accessed October 1, 2016, http://www.sap.com/6eyeopeningengagementstatistics, 2014; Selden, Sally, www.shrm.org, accessed October 1, 2016, http://www.shrm.org /qualityoftheirperformanceappraisalsystems, 2013.)

The "Real Work" of a Manager: Kathy and Brian

Kathy, the director of HR, has been trying to get Brian to complete his employee evaluations since he took over the marketing department 14 months ago. He always says he will get to it and yet he has not completed one evaluation for any of his department's 17 employees. Kathy is getting very upset with him, plus she is fearful that she and the company may get in trouble if any problems with Brian's employees were to occur.

Most of the workers in the department are patient and unconcerned about the situation (they are no more eager to get their evaluations than Brian is to give them), but there are six people who have repeatedly requested their evaluations. Brian keeps putting them and Kathy off under the guise of being too busy with other higher priority tasks. He also claims that the evaluations simply take too long to fill out. Kathy has offered to work with Brian to help him fill out the evaluations, and although he says this a good idea, nothing ever comes of it.

Brian has been through this before with nagging HR managers, who consistently want those evaluations filled out. He has learned, however, that if he just appeases them and tells them, he has every intention of getting around to the evaluations, that that usually satisfies them for months, if not years. Brian believes that preparing these evaluations and going through them one-on-one with the members of his team is not "real work." In his experience, these meetings do not accomplish anything, and they certainly don't improve his working relationship with his employees. Often, they make things worse because employees always expect a raise afterward, and if it is not forthcoming their performance gets even worse than it was before. In the past, Brian has found that just filling out each form takes an hour, plus another hour to blow through it with each employee. In short, to Brian, employee evaluations are just a colossal waste of everyone's time.

Manager Bias

When completing employee evaluations, managers naturally exhibit bias in their ratings. "Although subjectivity and partiality never will be completely removed from the process, it is important to keep some of our most common prejudices in mind when completing performance reviews" (HR Pros of the HR Support Center 2014).

Below is a "Top 10" list of the most frequent biases found in the employee evaluation process:

1. *Recency bias*: This occurs when the manager bases the evaluation on the last few weeks or months rather than the entire year or evaluation period. This is usually a result of a manager that does not take notes throughout the year and does a "last minute" appraisal of the employee.
2. *Halo effect*: This refers to the manager who remembers only one exceptional strength and allows it to carry over into other categories, or who tends to discount the bad because of a particular incident in the past. This effect can be harmful because the training or coaching provided can be minimal compared to the overall performance requirements of the employee. For example, if an employee excels in the category of "job knowledge," it does not necessarily follow that the employee excels in the categories of "attendance" or "work production."
3. *Similar-to-me bias*: As its name implies, this occurs when the manager gives better ratings to employees who are like the manager. Personal bias can play a role between a manager and an employee who have developed a friendly relationship, in that the manager is more likely to give that particular employee a more favorable evaluation than the employee may rightfully deserve.
4. *Opportunity bias*: This occurs when the manager either credits or faults the employee for factors beyond that employee's control. Managers afflicted with this bias praise or blame the employee for results when the actual cause of the performance was an opportunity or a lack thereof. As an example, consider a manager who gives a salesperson a favorable rating due to one big sale obtained by a stroke of luck, and less-favorable rating to one who may make several smaller sales regularly by reaching prospecting goals through constant cold calling. Which salesperson is more likely to achieve consistent success moving forward?
5. *Severity bias*: Managers tend to demonstrate this bias when attempting to motivate average-performing employees. "A manager with this bias tends to rate all employees lower than their performance warrants to inspire average employees to improve."
6. *Targeting bias*: This occurs when an employee has one hindering weakness, and the manager allows this to affect other categories or the overall outcome of the employee's evaluation. For example, if an employee is especially weak in the category of "sales prospecting," it is not necessarily true that the employee may need to make improvement in the categories

of "product knowledge" or "closing ratios." As much as possible, managers should judge performance categories independent of one another.

7. *Length-of-service bias*: Managers may have the tendency to remember only an employee's most recent performance, or to assume that a long-term employee is continuing to perform in the same fashion as in the past due to that person's length of service. Therefore, long-term employees should be evaluated according to the same established standards as other employees.

8. *Contrast bias*: "A manager afflicted with this bias tends to compare performance to other employees rather than comparing performance to an established company standard. It is important that the manager not consider the performance of other employees in an attempt to rank employees in the evaluation process" (HR Pros of the HR Support Center 2014). Every employee deserves his or her performance review to be based solely on individual performance, not performance as compared with other employees.

9. *Job vs. individual bias*: Some jobs seem more vital to the organization than others. "A particular job may be crucial to the company's success, but it does not necessarily follow that the employee is performing well in that critical role" (HR Pros of the HR Support Center 2014).

10. *Rating inflation*: Many managers cannot face their employees honestly and succumb to an inflated rating system for evaluations in which even the worst employees are rated as "fair" or "good" for several reasons, the simplest being that it is hard to tell someone that they are performing poorly. Thus, managers soften the actual reality of the evaluation and use "fair," "good," and "satisfactory" ratings as neutral terms to describe poor performance. However, managers are not concerned with lawsuits that, in their mind, will likely never happen. The problem, of course, is that lawsuits do happen and in such cases, a satisfactory evaluation will be taken to mean satisfactory performance, leaving the manager and the HR director scrambling for other evidence demonstrating that the employee performed poorly. Rating inflation also occurs because managers want to use the employee evaluation to motivate and improve the morale of employees, rather than a way to criticize poor performance. This is a prime example of poor manager development, which I will touch on later in this book. More to the point, positive but inaccurate evaluations may not have a motivating effect on problem employees. On the contrary, there is a high probability that such evaluations lower the bar for problem employees and encourage mediocre performance.

When a manager can remove some of the bias from the evaluation process, performance appraisals become much more meaningful for employee development, decision making, and compensation adjustments.

The Right and Wrong Way to Terminate:
Jenny, Mark, and Dylan

Mark is frustrated by his assistant Dylan's constant mistakes, slow progress, lies about needing time off, and coming in late, so he storms over to the office of Jenny, the company's director of HR.

"I have had it up to here with Dylan's incompetence, and I want to fire him immediately," he barks without preamble, as he bursts through Jenny's door.

"Have a seat," Jenny responds, motioning with an air of resignation to a chair facing her desk. "What has he done this time?"

"What hasn't he done?" Mark practically yells. "Everything about the guy is lackluster and shady. I am always making up for his mistakes and covering for him when he calls in sick or comes in late. Honestly, I cannot stand to look at him another day."

"OK. Have you documented your complaints, explained them to Dylan, made sure he understood the gravity of the situation and tried to train and coach him?"

Mark squirms in his seat. "Sure, I've documented some of them, and I've spoken with him about his poor performance, but he always has an excuse, so I gave up talking to him about it. I do have documentation of when he was late, and I wrote down when I found mistakes in his paperwork and all the times he needed extra time off for supposedly needing to go to the doctor."

"But did you speak with him specifically about these infractions, write them down and have him sign to indicate that you discussed everything?" Jenny asks. "Can you show that you trained and coached him on how to correct these mistakes?"

"Kinda," Mark says, feeling deflated.

Jenny promises to pull Dylan's file with Mark's notations and review it. The following day, she walks into Mark's office and closes the door.

"I looked over the documents on file, and they looked marginal at best, so I contacted our attorney," Jenny says. "Based on your documentation he advised against termination. You must go through the exact process we trained you on when you became a manager: document each serious infraction, have the employee sign it and then prove that you did your best to train, coach and counsel the right behaviors. Only then can we feel semiconfident that we can legally terminate and reduce our legal exposure."

"That is stupid and a waste of time!" Mark says, "How long do I have to do this?"

"Three to six months. Oh, and you cannot just single him out, or that will expose us as well."

"So employees have all the rights, huh?"

"I told you how to do it correctly, but you cut corners and didn't approach this properly," Jenny replies. "If you did we could probably be moving forward with terminating Dylan now."

Grounds for Employee Lawsuits

As mentioned above, managers bring their biases, whether conscious or subconscious, to the evaluation process. "Any of those listed above can be detrimental to an objective, legally defensible evaluation that is consistent with the employee's performance. It can also be legally problematic by being inconsistent with the organization's standards of performance" (Juniata 2011). A creative employee (or more likely, that employee's attorney) can use such inconsistences to prove that the employee was treated illegally as compared to other employees.

The following are some of the more conventional minefields that can cause litigation (VanBogaert n.d.):

- *Age discrimination*: An employee receiving an unfavorable evaluation could claim that the evaluation is a ploy for discrimination based on age in violation of the Age Discrimination Act.
- *Retaliation*: This typically occurs when a manager gives a negative evaluation to "get even" with an employee for a reason unrelated to job performance.
- *Discrimination*: The Civil Rights Act, Title VII, prohibits employers from discriminating against any individual by race, color, religion, gender, or national origin. State laws may include additional groups protected from discrimination in the workplace.

■ *Harassment*: Inappropriate questions and comments made to employees during the evaluation process may form the basis for harassment or discrimination complaints.

■ *Negligence*: "An employee may have a claim based on an employer's negligence in conducting, or failure to conduct, an employee evaluation. If the employee is not given a regularly scheduled evaluation, the employer may be held liable for negligence" (HR Pros of the HR Support Center 2014).

Because managers exercise broad discretion in the evaluation process, the opportunity for abuse exists. Evaluations, therefore, must guard against such abuse by maintaining consistency, objectivity, and relevance, particularly when an employee receives an evaluation resulting in an adverse employment action, e.g., denial of pay increase and/or job loss. Another valuable precautionary step to avoid legal challenges to negative evaluations is the training of managers. Because employers may be held liable for retaliatory or negligent negative evaluations by a manager, proper training of managers is important.

Evaluation programs, regardless of the method used, must be professionally administered. Evaluations should also be considered as significant potential evidence for an employer's defense. Properly documented evaluations build paper trails that favor employers in defending against lawsuits. Conversely, written comments in evaluations that are too general, taken out of context, ambiguous, or too lenient not only undermine subsequent discipline of a poor performer but also serve as ammunition for lawsuits by disgruntled former employees. Therefore, managers must be adequately trained to understand the essential criteria, as well as to minimize the employer's exposure to liability for wrongful terminations and related claims.

THE SMART APPROACH TO DEFENSIBLE EMPLOYEE ACCOUNTABILITY

Smart: defines specific outputs and/or results

Measurable: establishes quantitative and qualitative values or methods to allow for objective monitoring

Attainable: realistic expectations that can be completed within the guidelines

Relevant: expectations are related to the requirements of the current position

Time-bound: related to time when a project must be completed

Example

Employees Do Not Quit the Company; They Quit Their Bosses: John and Sam

John knew if he was going to have a good day or a bad day the moment he drove into the parking lot at work each morning. If the silver Volvo was parked in the corner under the big oak tree, it was going to be a long, grueling day of being ripped on by his boss Sam, the director of IT.

Sam meant well but believed in the "I do not talk to you unless you mess up" theory of management. Sam could always find something wrong with every install, security, or storage issue his techs worked on.

Sam believed that people learn best when their mistakes are pointed out so that they can be more easily corrected. "When I am riding someone it means I care," he said. "When I ignore them, it means they cannot learn, and they are on their way out."

Unfortunately, this kind of "caring" wasn't sufficient to keep John, who eventually went to work for a competitor across town. Sam was shocked when John quit because he considered him one of his best techs. However, John had quit precisely because of Sam, not the company as a whole or because of any friction with other employees or clients. In fact, it was just the opposite. Over the years, John had created good friendships among his coworkers and customers, but it was not enough to keep him given the relentless mistreatment delivered by Sam.

Everyone needs professional development that provides an honest and objective assessment of his or her strengths as well as his or her blind spots, especially managers. If you are a manager, ask a trusted colleague or mentor for their advice, or hire a consultant or coach to work with you. People need to hear the truth and then take consistent steps to improve, or their careers will stall. Superstars in every vocation and sport relentlessly act to improve their skills with the help of a qualified coach or mentor, and it should be no different for business managers.

Results of Poor Handling of Employee Evaluations and the Myth of Teamwork

When employee evaluations are handled poorly, people retaliate in one way or another. At the very least, "people feel unappreciated. They become more conservative. They set their goals low to ensure that they are seen as succeeding. They retreat from candid conversations about development because the whole issue of progress and feedback is so emotionally charged. The experience becomes one of a ticking time bomb" (Rock 2014). "It leads to employees focusing on competing with each other rather than competing with other companies. A similar unintended consequence occurs up the hierarchy. If employees feel that their bosses are comparing them against their peers, they will not openly share information that might compromise their ranking" (Rock 2014). In today's hypercompetitive environment, people working together are essential for business success. By focusing on the individual and their performance in isolation, we often miss the opportunity to improve team cohesion and cooperation.

Pay someone to be excellent and you often open the door to competitive and dysfunctional behavior resulting in conscious or subconscious sabotage. Employees find ways of undermining their "competitors" through rumor-mongering, not sharing useful information, and manipulating goals and measures (i.e., underpromising and overdelivering). Rewarding employees financially is often a counterproductive way of encouraging cooperation toward a common purpose. Ego, status, and feel-good triggers all too often motivate employees who work for monetary rewards, which take the eye off the right priority: intrinsic motivation, finding meaning in one's work, being part of a larger whole, and developing a cohesive, winning team.

How Do We Fix It? What Are the Next Steps?

Now we move from what is wrong with the employee evaluation process and focus our sights on how to be more efficient at developing people. The next chapter will clearly show that a transparent give-and-take management and employee review system in which employees understand the criteria, standards, and process is imperative. In fact, enthusiastic and sustained employee participation in the development and administration of the review process is required for success. This only enhances employee acceptance and commitment to the review process while lowering their stress and apprehension.

"Participation is promoted by self-appraisals, joint development of performance goals and standards, and active solicitation of employee input during the manager and employee development process. Another key element is the adoption of a performance coaching model in which managers help employees develop present and future job skills and employ a joint problem-solving approach to issues involving performance" (Roberts and Pregitzer 2007).

Summary

One reason why performance appraisal in organizations is emotionally resisted so strongly is that managers know full well they are violating the larger cultural rules and norms when they sit a subordinate down to give him or her 'feedback.' To put it bluntly, when we tell people what we 'really think of them' in an aggressive way, this can be functionally equivalent to social murder. Someone going around and doing this is viewed as unsafe to have around, and, if the behavior persists, we often declare such a person mentally ill and lock him or her up.

The responses listed below are from actual employees who have had trouble understanding the value of the current employee evaluation model:

1. Managers do not know their employees.
2. Managers are not trained properly.
3. In evaluations, there is a thin line between the person and that person's performance. Employee evaluations can turn personal very fast. Managers do not know how to conduct a proper employee evaluation.
4. The process is time-consuming for managers.

Below is a "Top 5" list of the most frequent biases found in the employee evaluation process:

1. Recency bias
2. Halo effect
3. Similar-to-me bias
4. Opportunity bias
5. Severity bias

DEVELOPING
THE PERSON

Chapter 3

From Being Hired to Adding Value in 90 Days or Less

Human behavior is extensively motivated and regulated through the exercise of self-influence. Among the mechanisms of self-influence, none is more focal or pervading than belief in one's personal efficacy. Unless people believe that they can produce desired effects and forestall undesired ones by their actions, they have little incentive to act or to persevere in the face of difficulties. Whatever other factors may serve as guides and motivators, they are rooted in the core belief that one has the power to produce desired results. To be an agent is to influence intentionally one's functioning and life conditions. In this view, people are contributors to their life circumstances, not just products of them.

Albert Bandura

Structural paths influence perceived self-efficacy and positively or negatively affect motivation and performance attainment. Managers and other major influencers can impede or assist goals and outcome expectations (Figure 3.1).

Social cognitive theory, as defined by psychologist Albert Bandura, refers to "self-efficacy as one's belief in one's ability to succeed in specific situations or accomplish a task. One's sense of self-efficacy can play a significant role in how one approaches goals, tasks, and challenges" (Ormrod 2006).

"Social learning theory describes the acquisition of skills that are developed exclusively or primarily within a social group. Social learning depends on how

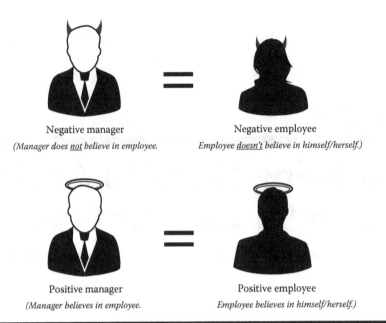

Negative manager
(Manager does <u>not</u> believe in employee.

Negative employee
Employee <u>doesn't</u> believe in himself/herself.)

Positive manager
(Manager believes in employee.

Positive employee
Employee believes in himself/herself.)

Figure 3.1 Structural paths.

individuals either succeed or fail at dynamic interactions within groups, and promotes the development of individual emotional and practical skills as well as an accurate perception of self and acceptance of others. According to this theory, people learn from one another through observation, imitation, and modeling. Self-efficacy reflects an individual's understanding of what skills he or she can offer in a group setting" (Ormrod 1999, *Human Learning* 3rd ed).

Getting Hired: What Happens during an Employee's First Week

When a new employee gets hired, he or she goes through very predictable patterns of thoughts and behaviors, which require the manager to adapt his or her management style to gain maximum trust and communicate so that performance can be leveraged to the fullest. Let's start with the feelings and thoughts new employees often exhibit.

Feelings and Thoughts

The primary emotions for a new employee are excitement and anticipation, coupled with anxiety and perhaps even a bit of fear at the prospect of figuring out a new manager and fitting into a new social structure or department. Along with these will be a feeling of pride at being chosen for this position over the other candidates. Once these initial feelings and thoughts run their course, the next phase of internal dialogue that generally presents itself includes

- Why am I here?
- Why are they here?
- What is expected of me?
- How much influence will I have?
- How much influence will my manager and my colleagues have over me?

Observable Behaviors

Anticipating and being aware of behaviors provides a relatively accurate road map into the mental patterns of the employee. Knowing these indicators helps the manager have a higher probability of choosing from various management styles to ensure successful integration of the employee into the organization. It is imperative for the manager to be just one-half step ahead of the new employee regarding training and behavior development. This awareness makes it much easier for the employee to keep up and follow the manager's lead, and much easier for the manager to quickly make midcourse adjustments.

A high degree of politeness will be one of these observable behaviors, perhaps with a touch of standoffishness. This guards the new employee against the unknown. Reserved interaction with the manager and sporadic participation with others in his or her group is also reasonable. At this point, the employee is extremely agreeable and will have an acute need for the manager to precisely define tasks, along with clear expectations and time limits for their completion. Being very specific reduces anxiety for the employee and provides necessary structure in the early phases of his or her immersion into the new organization.

Employee Needs

From the very beginning, define the big picture for your new employee. Does the organization or department have a mission? Providing this overarching vision works as a beacon, giving the person a stable goal orientation. Remember, he or she is coming into the new organization primarily "culture blind." Even if he or she is a specialist and knows their skills very well, there will almost certainly be a lack of awareness of the cultural norms with which the organization and department (as well as the manager) operate. The new employee requires

- Very clear goals and objectives
- A measurement system and precise timeline
- Knowledge about when feedback is expected and in what form
- Well-defined roles and responsibilities, both personally and for the broader department or team

Management Style and Requirements

At this stage, the manager must first establish trust and communication through dialogue. One idea that works very well to break the ice is to ask the employee to share one or two hobbies or non-work-related topics that he or she knows well enough to teach others. Ask for a three-minute example. This provides insightful information that aids in relaxing the employee and allowing him or her to talk and the manager to listen. Most of the time a new employee's time is spent listening and being overwhelmed with new information, so being encouraged to share in this way reduces anxiety, increases bonding, and provides the manager with the employee's learning preference. This relates to the general systems theory, which has a powerful use in a business setting.

General systems theory, developed by biologist Ludwig Von Bertalanffy, states that knowing one part of a system enables us to know something about another part. A cross-sectional approach deals with understanding the patterns between the two systems. Once known, systems thinking can be applied to all types of systems. Said another way, general systems theory states that learning can be made much easier, and subsequently quicker if the manager attaches new material to the employee's previously known material. In this manner, the person simply unpackages the metaphor he or she is already familiar with (e.g., golf, tennis, knitting, etc.) and adds the new skill to his or her mental filing system. All of us speak in metaphor, and it's invaluable to learn the subordinate's metaphors. If the person uses golf, then explain new lessons using golf metaphors; if skiing is the chosen sport, then reference skiing when explaining a new concept or task.

General systems theory tunes the manager into listening, and it is through listening that the manager can genuinely understand how to quickly and correctly manage a new employee and get a quicker return on the investment in that person. Building on general systems theory and taking it a step further allows one to build on the power of metaphor.

Metaphors are an excellent way of taking something known and comparing it to something unknown. If you use your words in this way, you could make difficult concepts clearer to those who might be struggling to understand them. For instance, people often get into a hurry and the faster they go the more mistakes they make. Thus, using a metaphor related to a hobby or sport the employee is intimately familiar with can help bridge this gap.

For example, let's assume the employee John gets his work done quickly but sloppily, with significant gaps in his research. During discussions around this issue, his boss Mike must provide additional guidance, do the research himself, or send John back to do it over. Mike has told John to slow down and think it through, but this hasn't been effective. Another way for Mike to coach John would be to utilize John's love of golf. Mike might say, "What steps must a golfer take before he hits a drive off the tee?" John would then begin to describe addressing the ball with the correct stance, focusing on the backswing, keeping eyes on the ball, leading with the hips, guiding the club with the leading arm, and driving through the ball. Only when all of this is done properly and in the right sequence, with the right timing, can the ball be hit accurately with the desired distance. Mike might respond by saying something like, "So what you're telling me is that preparation beforehand is far more important than the actual act of hitting the ball?" When John agrees, Mike can use these steps as his metaphor to explain the preparation John must undertake before completing a project. In this way, Mike is helping John take something he knows and applying it to a new concept.

Learning Preferences

How, exactly, do different employees learn? Developing employees and helping them execute properly is possibly the most important thing one can do as a manager. By presenting material in a variety of different ways, one can appeal to employees who understand and learn in a variety of ways. One way that one can differentiate development is by appealing to different modalities (primarily, appealing to different senses). The three primary modalities that managers need to be aware of and focus on are visual, auditory, and kinesthetic (VAK).

Visual, Auditory, and Kinesthetic Learning Styles (VAK) (University of Pennsylvania 2009). The VAK learning model, developed by Walter Burke Barbe and colleagues, employs three primary sensory receivers: visual, auditory, and kinesthetic (movement) to determine an individual's dominant learning style. "It is sometimes known as VAKT (visual, auditory, kinesthetic, and tactile). It is based on modalities—channels by which human expression can take place and is composed of a combination of perception and memory."

VAK is derived from the accelerated learning world and is a very popular current model due to its simplicity. Although research has shown a connection between modalities and learning styles the research has so far been unable to prove that using one's learning style provides the best means for learning a task or subject. This is probably because it is more of preference, rather than a style. Figure 3.2 shows a statistical breakdown of the five senses regarding how people best learn: Visual, Auditory, and Kinesthetic Learning Styles (VAK) (Clark 2009).

Employees mainly use the top three modalities to receive and integrate new information and experiences. However, according to the VAK or modality theory, one or two of these receiving styles is typically dominant. This dominant style defines the best way for an employee to learn new information by filtering what is to be learned. This style may not have to always be the same for some tasks. The employee may prefer one style of learning for one task, and a combination of others for a different task.

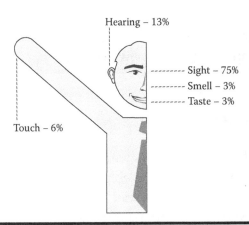

Figure 3.2   Learning styles VAK.

Recognizing and Implementing the Three VAK Styles

Visual learners have two subchannels—linguistic and spatial. Employees who are visual–linguistic like to learn through written language, such as reading and writing tasks. They remember what has been written down, even if they do not read it more than once. They like to write down directions and pay better attention to discussions or lectures if they watch them. Employees who are visual–spatial usually have difficulty with the written language and do better with charts, demonstrations, videos, and other visual materials. They easily visualize faces and places by using their imagination and seldom get lost in new surroundings. To integrate this style into the learning environment, the manager should use "Visual, Auditory, and Kinesthetic Learning Styles (VAK)" (Clark 2009).

- Use graphs, charts, illustrations, or other visual aids.
- Include outlines, concept maps, agendas, handouts, etc. for reading and taking notes.
- Include plenty of content in handouts to reread after the learning session.
- Leave white space in handouts for note-taking.
- Invite questions to help employees stay alert in auditory environments.
- Post flip charts to show what will come and what has been presented.
- Emphasize key points to cue when to take notes.
- Eliminate potential distractions.
- Supplement textual information with illustrations whenever possible.
- Encourage employees draw meaningful images in the margins.
- Have employees visualize the topic and/or mentally rehearse the process or subject matter.

Auditory learners often talk to themselves. They also may move their lips and read out loud. They may otherwise have difficulty with reading and/or writing tasks. They often do better talking to a colleague and hearing what was said. To integrate this style into the learning environment, the manager should

- Begin new material with a brief explanation of what is coming. Conclude with a summary of what has been covered. This is the old adage of "tell them what they are going to learn, teach them, and show them what they have learned."

- Use the Socratic method of discussion, teaching, or coaching. This involves closely questioning employees to draw as much information from them as possible, and then (when necessary) to fill in the gaps with your own expertise.
- Include auditory activities, such as brainstorming and discussion. Leave plenty of time to debrief discussions and projects. This allows employees to make connections between what they learned and how it applies to their situation.
- Have the employees verbalize the questions.
- Develop an internal dialogue between yourself and the employee.

"Kinesthetic learners do best while touching and moving. It also has two subchannels: kinesthetic (movement) and tactile (touch)" (University of Pennsylvania 2009). Such learners tend to lose concentration if there is little or no external stimulation or movement. "When listening to discussions they may want to take notes for the sake of moving their hands. When reading, they like to scan the material first, and then focus in on the details (get the big picture first). They typically use color highlighters and take notes by drawing pictures, diagrams, or doodling. To integrate this style into the learning environment, the manager should

- Use activities that get the employees up and moving.
- Play music, when appropriate, during activities.
- Use colored markers to emphasize key points on flip charts or white boards.
- Give frequent stretch breaks (brain breaks).
- Provide them the parts or other work-related objects to give them something to do with their hands.
- Provide highlighters, colored pens, and/or pencils.
- Guide employees through a visualization of complex tasks.
- Have them transfer information from the text or manual to another medium such as a keyboard or a tablet."

Management Style and Requirements

In integrating this information into a management style, a manager must be very direct and clear as to what is expected by the organization. By no means does this mean to scare or intimidate the new employee—just the opposite. Every organization has their cultural norms and now is the time to share them.

For example, I once worked with a CEO who held Monday morning meetings that started precisely at 8:00 a.m. sharp. At 8, the door was closed and locked. If you didn't make it to the Monday morning meeting by then you simply weren't involved. Obviously timeliness was critical in this company. All organizations and managers have their do's and don'ts and the manager must teach the new employee the correct way right from the start. Do not leave this for the employee to learn on his or her own or from the grapevine. Many people within the organization may have a distorted view of the organization if it is at an unhealthy point in its evolution, and the grapevine will share the positive, the negative, and the made-up.

To overcome this, be proactive. Be very clear and tell the person

- What to do.
- When to do it and when it will be due. Be precise and say things like, "next Thursday at 3:00 p.m.," as opposed to, "the middle of next week."
- Where they need to be at certain times.
- How to specifically complete tasks.
- With whom they should work and who to stay clear of.

This may seem like overkill but I have seen people get sabotaged by the most obscure individuals and events. Once a new employee gets off track, it takes twice the time to correct the imbalance and reteach. Do it right the first time and save yourself and your new employee a lot of unnecessary difficulties.

Week 1 through the End of the First Month

Let's suppose an employee was hired on Monday. By Friday afternoon, at the end of the first week, the manager should meet with the employee and do a quick review. This should be considered as a coaching opportunity for both the employee and the manager, with an eye toward the accomplishment of four goals. First, the employee needs to know what he or she has been doing well and where improvements or clarifications are required. Second, the manager needs input on how he or she can better manage, guide, and develop the employee. Third, this establishes a dynamic whereby regular training and coaching is standard and part of the culture. And fourth, this solidifies communication and trust between the manager and the employee. These four points are at the heart of any great manager–employee relationship and the foundation that separates great organizations from mediocre ones.

This week-ending review is typically a six-step process, as follows:

1. Start by asking the employee to meet at 3:00 p.m. on Friday afternoon. Make the meeting conversational in nature and start out with general questions relating to the work, the people, and navigating the office environment.
2. Move the conversation toward specific behaviors and tasks that went surprisingly well and reinforce these.
3. Address the behaviors and duties that missed the mark. There is no need to demean or talk down to the employee; remember, this meeting is intended to be conversational in nature. Don't forget that the person has only been employed five days! Simply reinforce that you want very much for the employee to be successful, and for that to happen it is necessary for learning to be frequent and accurate.
4. Next, ask what you can do to help this person be more successful. Be aware that 99% of employees have never experienced this type of question before (especially after the first week on the job), so he or she will need to be encouraged to provide the input so that the balance of power is equalized. A quick word about ego: Don't ever forget that the job of an employee is to successfully complete certain assigned duties every day. The manager's job is to manage and guide the development of people and groups of people. That's it. So, eliminate your ego here and encourage him or her to teach and coach you so that you can manage the person to the best of your abilities. Obviously, there should be no defiance or insubordination by either the employee or the manager. Both have a job to do if the department and the organization are to be successful.
5. At the end of this meeting the manager should have clearly defined a set of goals for the following week. Again, these need to be specific duties with timelines and measurements built in.
6. Keep in mind that developing people is time-consuming at the very beginning, but as the weeks and months go by, it takes less and less time to gain more and more value from each of your direct reports. Stick with it and you will reap the great rewards that being a superstar

manager gains, namely, that you will be "lucky" enough to be sur-
rounded by superstar employees. This is a proven method of outshining
colleagues and competitors alike.

Weeks 2 and 3

Duplicate in weeks two and three what you did in week one. Each meeting
should become easier for both parties, and the expectations for each should
increase. Remember, a manager's job is to develop employees by training
and coaching them, again, staying just one-half step ahead so you don't lose
them on the journey toward your mutual success. Many people don't see
it this way except for the high-end professional, who understands that the
employee–manager relationship is an actual team sport. One cannot be successful without the other. In fact, when an employee fails, the manager must
shoulder at least 30%–40% of the blame. Why? Generally, because of at least
one of the six following reasons:

1. You hired the wrong person for your management style.
2. You hired the wrong person for the organizational culture.
3. You hired the wrong person for the team they would be working with.
4. You didn't learn how to leverage the person's skills and/or reduce their
   limitations quickly enough.
5. You were reluctant to immediately and honestly address task, communication, or process shortfalls.
6. You didn't encourage the person to be totally honest with you, possibly
   because your ego is not strong enough to learn from those you manage.
   Look, for an NFL team to make it to the Super Bowl, the quarterback
   and wide receivers should work as one unit, not two separate entities.
   When one fails to either throw or catch the ball, the whole team loses
   ground.

Conversely, the employee must shoulder the responsibility for the
other 60%–70% of success or failure. The better a manager becomes at
working closely with an employee and applying these skills, the clearer
this lesson will become and the more successful the manager will be in
his or her career. There will be a direct and robust correlation between
implementing these lessons and a manager's rise in the organization.
The manager's superiors will notice how quickly his or her employees

perform vs. others, and start giving that manager larger and tougher problems to solve. Everything executed within business at all levels is done with and through people. If one knows how to manage people effectively, that manager understands how to leverage the strength of many. This is a rare quality and one that is highly regarded and financially reimbursed.

Succeeding as an Introverted Manager: Timid Tami

Tami was the manager of an accounting department. Although she was accomplished at her job, the managing of people had proven difficult for her. She was incredibly kind, to the point where people could and did take advantage of her. Tami knew this about herself but was too hesitant to speak up for fear of hurting someone's feelings.

This department needed another accountant so we went through the process outlined to develop both Tami and her newly hired assistant. Tami and I made a list of topics that her new employee should be able to learn within the first weeks' time. We practiced them and then shared them with the new employee and told her we would be reviewing her performance Friday afternoon at 3:00 p.m. When Friday came, Timid Tami was concerned but we did the review together. The new accountant had done very well overall but needed more attention to detail when doing receivables.

Due to outside forces in the new employee's life, she had also been late a few times and her husband would wait in the parking lot, which created problems when the work couldn't be finished at exactly 5:00 p.m. Tami brought this up by saying, "I know you have had personal challenges lately but I would like for you to be to work on time and I'm concerned that your husband is expecting you to be out at precisely 5:00 p.m. This is a problem because we cannot always be done at 5:00 p.m. sharp."

I asked the employee if this was OK and she said, "Yes, I totally understand." I then asked the employee how she would like Tami to speak to her in the future. Much to Tami's surprise, the employee said she would like Tami to be much more direct and not hesitate to tell her what she wanted. The three of us debriefed this and went over how Tami and the new employee felt about all of this. Afterward, when Tami and I debriefed the meeting, she said it was very "eye-opening" to learn that she needed to speak up and be more straightforward. We practiced every Friday and by the end of the month they both had improved significantly with the work as well as the communication between them. Tami's confidence at speaking up in the moment had improved by an enormous margin as well.

The 30-Day Mark

The most critical time for establishing favorable behavior is in the first 30 days. The second most important time to establish behavior is between 30 and 90 days. It is within this period that people will start to deviate from established patterns if they haven't been developed properly to adhere to the cultural norms of the department, colleagues, and the manager. During this time, it is essential that the manager provides goals and expectations for the employee, his or her role, the quality and volume of work, and resource allocation. Group communication and collaboration should be improving consistently during this time as well. The manager and the employee should be used to trusting, communicating, and coaching one another and so pre-scheduled weekly meetings won't be necessary. In its place, these learning and coaching moments could occur naturally as needed, for instance, while passing in the hallway.

Training Programs

Managers have a significant effect on the morale and productivity of their department and the organization. However, they are often selected for their technical competencies and job-related knowledge, whereas their success in managing others is primarily based on their interpersonal skills to guide, enable, and motivate those they manage.

Weak and/or rushed training programs often rely on hype or are heavy on rules. Any motivational effects quickly dissipate as the initial burst of enthusiasm fades. Unfortunately, the methods most widely used in today's organizations are often the least effective, but because they are easy and cheap to administer, they continue to be used. I will outline empirically tested processes for training, which will be slightly costlier up front but prove to produce a much higher and long-term return on investment and significantly improve performance.

"Management using guided mastery skills effectively have been shown to improve the morale, problem-solving skills, had a significant lower rate of absenteeism, lower turnover of employees and a 17% increase in the monthly level of productivity over a six-month period" (Bandura 2009, pp. 179–200).

Physical Guided Mastery

The most effective way of developing employees is through social modeling and skill proficiency, with gradual increases in possible anxiety/pressure. Competent models convey knowledge, skills, and strategies for managing tasks. By their example, the models temporarily provide not only how to do a task but also spark interest in achievement and prove that ordinary people can be successful through training. Hearing of similar employees who confronted and overcome difficulties in learning new skills can significantly improve the new employee's confidence that he or she too can learn to be successful.

Subskill Development

Complex skills are made easier when they are broken down into subskills. This produces better retention than trying to teach everything at once. After the subskills are learned, they can be combined into complex strategies to serve different purposes. Efficient modeling teaches general rules and strategies for dealing with various situations rather than specific scripted responses or routines. People who learn standards in the abstract and learn from a list taught in a passive classroom context generally do a very poor job at applying them and making them part of their everyday routine. The modeling must mirror the daily routine to be most effective.

Learning from Mistakes

Success is often achieved by learning from mistakes. Therefore, resilience training must be built by training how to manage failure so that it is informative rather than demoralizing.

"The feedback that is most effective and achieves the greatest improvement takes the form of corrective modeling. In this approach, the subskills that have not been adequately learned are further modeled and learners rehearse them until they are mastered.

"Many of the problems of occupational functioning reflect failures of self-management rather than deficiencies of knowledge and technical abilities" (Bandura 2009, pp. 179–200). An important aspect of competency development must include training in being resilient to difficulties. Many managers create more conflict and problems than they correct because they get frustrated at a new employee who doesn't learn skills quickly enough. The manager then admonishes the employee in a futile attempt to make him or her concentrate and work harder. Unfortunately, this is akin to the prevailing management philosophy of the thirteenth century: "The beatings will continue until morale improves." Said another way: it's very easy to destroy an employee's will and desire to learn and trust; All one must do is simply punish optimism.

From Basic Training to Personal Development: Brandon and Tim

Tim had been promoted from warehouse worker to assistant manager in a shipping and receiving department. The challenges that Tim and his manager Brandon both shared were in developing a larger team of people. They both progressed to their positions by working harder than others and being enthusiastic. Both were natural leaders who lead by example. This management style works fine if one is leading two or three people, but when the numbers get into the thirty-plus range, then developing the whole person is mandatory.

Brandon had to learn how to transition from a working manager to a thinking manager who was more strategic in his involvement with employees. We talked about developing the whole person, and spending time thinking, observing, talking with employees, encouraging good work, and talking with employees who were not hitting the mark. At first this proved to be tough for Brandon, but now he had an assistant manager who needed to learn the same skills or they would both fall behind.

The three of us met and made monthly, weekly, and daily objectives for the manufacturing operation based on production needs. At first it was difficult for them to go through this process because they didn't see it as working but "just talking." We stuck with it, however, and soon they realized that their jobs were to observe, teach, coach, and counsel their employees. In addition, their job was to encourage and model successful behaviors, help employees learn from failure, and address problems immediately. Every so often when they were needed to jump in to help, they were able to teach by example. When this occurred, they received even more respect from the employees.

Between Day 30 and 75

During the first month or two, the new employee and the established employees will go through a natural recalibration of the pecking order. The new employee may feel resistant to certain people and tasks, and his or her attitude will likely fluctuate. The person is becoming a part of the natural culture and his or her normal behaviors are starting to surface.

The astute manager may notice defensiveness and competition among certain colleagues as power struggles emerge. If not handled quickly, performance can take a backseat to the possible conflict among members. The best way to overcome this is to immediately address the interpersonal nature of the team and acknowledge the normal tendency for this to happen. In fact, it must occur when new members join a group. By normalizing this situation and addressing it as a stage of development rather than something "wrong," the manager can help remove the power of conflict and can more effectively restore the team to a state of equilibrium.

The wise manager facilitates a conversation about the various personalities and how each one is required for the team to evolve and grow. People need to share their similarities as well as their differences and learn to listen to one another. They are in a perfect position to teach one another about their upbringing, their personal culture, and the organizational culture, and to clarify misperceptions or previously misworded statements. During this time, the manager guides the team through these minefields by supporting the individuals but also asking how they can solve problems among themselves with mutual support. The key is to encourage relationship-building while providing clear expectations and task-oriented goals.

Other key factors to be considered are

- The influence of the grapevine—it can be positive for a healthy organization, or negative for a dysfunctional one.
- Is the manager providing the time necessary for training and coaching to ensure employee and team success?

Between 75 and 90 Days

If you haven't already done so, by the third month the manager must determine if the new hire will stay with the organization or if it be best for him or her to transition out of the organization. (HR rules and restrictions differ from state to state so get legal assistance regarding the 90-day trial period.)

Questions to consider at this point include the following:

- Is trust and collaboration among the manager, the employee, and the team improving?
- Can the employee follow direction?
- Does the employee add to, take away from, or provide little value during meetings, brainstorming, and debriefing sessions?
- Is the person a solid A, B, or C employee? What does the team and position require? What do you require of them?
- This is the time to decide whether to keep or terminate the employee. It's not the time to be wishy-washy and reticent. One must be bold and think first about how to improve the team and organization.
- As a manager, perform a self-assessment: Did you give the employee the necessary time or did you shortchange that person?
- If you must terminate, what will you do different to improve when you make your next hire?

This chapter addressed how to develop new employees. In the next chapter, we will turn our attention toward developing long-term employees through the principles of the MED Review.

Summary

"Human behavior is extensively motivated and regulated through the exercise of self-influence. Among the mechanisms of self-influence, none is more focal or pervading than belief in one's personal efficacy. Unless people believe that they can produce desired effects and forestall undesired ones by their actions, they have little incentive to act or to persevere in the face of difficulties. Whatever other factors may serve as guides and motivators, they are rooted in the core belief that one has the power to produce desired results. To be an agent is to influence intentionally one's functioning and life conditions. In this view, people are contributors to their life circumstances, not just products of them" (Bandura 2009, pp. 179–200).

Let's suppose an employee was hired on Monday. By Friday afternoon, at the end of the first week, the manager should meet with the employee and do a quick review. This should be considered as a coaching opportunity for both the employee and the manager, with an eye toward the accomplishment of four goals. First, the employee needs to know what he or she has been doing well and where improvements or clarifications are required. Second, the manager needs input on how he or she can better manage, guide, and develop the employee. Third, this establishes a dynamic whereby regular training and coaching is standard and part of the culture. And fourth, this solidifies communication and trust between the manager and the employee. These four points are at the heart of any great manager–employee relationship and the foundation that separates great organizations from mediocre ones.

Chapter 4

Great Reviews Start with Great Communication

Do you know what separates great organizations from good ones? The answer is effective and dynamic interpersonal communication skills. Successful managers at winning organizations understand the value generated by employees who take the time to fully interact with and understand one another.

Effective communication skills, therefore, are foundational in building successful business relationships. Effective communication doesn't just happen, however. It is a learned skill that needs continuous updating and refinement, and great managers will encourage, nurture, and reward this behavior in their direct reports. This takes desire, discipline, practice, and consistent effort over time so that it becomes a habit, but the effort is well worth it.

There are some straightforward ways to address this complex reality. You can begin by understanding the fallacies and pitfalls inhibiting successful communications. This will help you become more aware of how people communicate, which is a critical skill for your personal managerial development.

When people talk to one another, in addition to the actual words being uttered, there are simultaneously many nonverbal messages being conveyed. Feelings and body language attach themselves in messages that are often subtle and sometimes hard to read, but which strongly influence the content and meaning of every message we send or receive. Recognizing and understanding these nonverbal cues is essential for successful communication to occur.

Tone and Body Language

The tone used in delivering a message affects its meaning. Beginning a statement with the words, "I thought I told you…" may be innocuous if those words are spoken with an easygoing tone or neutral inflection of your voice, and delivered with even spacing or timing on each word. On the other hand, those same first five words, spoken using an impatient, angry, or chilly tone, with an emphasis on a particular word, or with varied word spacing or timing, can considerably change the meaning and implication of the words to follow.

Meanwhile, body movements or positions, hand gestures, facial expressions, and eye contact (or lack of eye contact) become the human punctuation marks from which the person receiving the message gathers significant information. In many cases, that person will remember how, when, where, why, and from whom the message was delivered with greater clarity than the actual content itself.

Four Barriers to Great Communication

1. *Mind reading.* Never assume you know what the other person is thinking. Ask. Be specific. People who work together a lot can often guess accurately as much as 90% of the time, but misunderstanding even 10% of the time is enough to ruin a team.
2. *Storing up annoyances and grievances.* It is better to express minor annoyances or concerns as they occur rather than store and "dump" them all at once. Even though the initial incident may have been minor, allowing frustration to build may lead to major arguments, and even derail a project or ruin a partnership.
3. *Withholding relevant negative information.* Sometimes people don't talk about important topics because they are afraid of making waves or upsetting an employee or manager. This often inadvertently leads to deceit and manipulation, which may in turn magnify an already unstable situation. Successful managers solve problems in the fastest and least disruptive way. The quicker a problem is "on the table,"

the quicker it can be resolved, and the quicker everyone can return to being productive.

4. *Using put-downs, certain kinds of humor and other disrespectful behaviors.* In arguments or disagreements, stick to the point. Focus on the current situation and never "hit below the belt." In every interaction, there are two messages. The first and most obvious message is the content itself. These are the facts, goals, and topic at hand. The second and more powerful message is the way in which the content is delivered. It is here where the danger lurks. The style of one's communication may cause considerably more damage to team members and the organization than the actual content of the message. You have no doubt heard sayings such as "It's not what you say, but how you say it," or "Think before you speak." These may be old sayings, but they remain in use for a good reason: they're relevant.

Seven Ways to Create Great Communication

1. *Keep your messages clear and consistent.* Be aware of the feelings that correspond with the content of what you are saying. Be sure that what you say, how you say it, and your body language all communicate the same message. Your words may lie, but your body language will always tell the truth.

2. *Use the other person's words, metaphors, and analogies.* Like behavior, language follows a pattern of redundancy, and people tend to use the same words over and again. Listen for their use of words as if it were a foreign language, because it often is. Moreover, people often use metaphors and analogies to describe events (e.g., "that was a home run" or "we dropped the ball on that one"). Listen for these turns of phrases, and once you have found a common theme, remember it. Then, simply translate your message in the language of the receiver's metaphor and deliver it back to them. For example, you might ask, "What specific lessons might we learn from this 'home run' that we could apply to other clients or customers?" or "What steps might we take next time so we don't 'drop the ball' with that client?" By utilizing this technique, the receiver doesn't have to decipher your metaphor, only the one new piece of information housed within it.

3. *Pay attention and listen carefully.* Focus on the other person and take the time to understand what he or she is saying. When it comes to

listening, go slow and you will accomplish more—i.e., you'll succeed quicker. Ask questions, listen closely, and observe the one with whom you are communicating. Both parties in a conversation need to be very specific. If you don't understand a word, ask the other person to define it. If a person uses a vague phrase, ask for specifics. For example, if your supervisor says, "I need you to be more professional," request a clarification of the word "professional." Request examples. When giving examples, on the other hand, speak to specific behaviors or actions that you have seen, and/or statements that you yourself have heard. These are measurable and precise.

4. *Develop trust.* During a discussion, both parties must have constructive motives. When you are delivering a message, you must first communicate to the receiver that you are trustworthy and genuinely interested in helping. On the other hand, when you are on the receiving end, you must demonstrate that you are present and actively listening. Avoid multitasking.

5. *Let people know that you understand their point of view.* Realize, however, that understanding a certain point of view does not necessarily mean that you agree with it. Many arguments consist of two people who feel misunderstood trying to get their point across to the other person repeatedly. This can quickly degenerate into a circular argument.

6. *Speak for yourself.* You can do this by using "I" statements rather than "you" statements. It's easier to communicate with a person who says, "I feel really upset by how this meeting is going" than with a person who says, "You always fly off the handle and yell at me whenever I try to tell you anything contrary to your point of view." "You" statements are like finger-pointing, and often encourage people to respond in a defensive and hostile manner. As a result, the receiver will likely shut down, get defensive in return, and not contribute in the future. Or worse, they will openly or covertly go underground and sabotage the team's best laid plans.

7. *Don't hog.* Let other people have their say. I will go one step further and advise you to encourage other people to express their opinions or ideas. Often people stop listening to what is being said, and are either reduced to muttering "uh-huh" response, or, at the other end of the spectrum, frequently interrupting to get their point across. Managers who regularly flaunt superior knowledge with their employees will get short-term results, but will be resented and, in the end, will have a weaker and overly dependent team. If you hear yourself saying,

"Can't anyone around here, make a decision besides me?" that result is likely because you have trained them to shut up and follow orders. If you want to improve your organization and career, you would be wise to encourage them to open up and share their ideas. They may not trust you at first, but if you are consistent and honest with them about your past tendency to "hog," they will slowly become the assets you hired them to be.

"If They Say Anything I Don't Like, I'm Quitting": Dave and SB Farms

In a career spanning more than 25 years at SB Farms, Dave hadn't been evaluated even one time. Neither had the other employees, and as a result, things had gotten very loose with the company. Production targets weren't being met, there was poor accountability and responsibility, employees were arriving late and not calling in when "sick," to name just a few.

I was brought in by the CEO to address these issues. He wanted to quickly tighten up the organization, make it run more smoothly, and of course generate more money. I recommended the manager and employee development review (MED Review), a system that I developed to teach and coach people to be more accountable. Far from a one-sided employee evaluation (which I believe is the worst thing ever invented for improving performance), the MED Review is based on open communication between both parties.

Dave was the maintenance manager for this corporate family farming organization. When we informed him that we'd be starting the MED Review process with him, he immediately asked, "Is that like an employee evaluation?"

"In a sense," I said, "But this is a totally different experience. You'll actually enjoy it."

We scheduled our initial meeting for Tuesday morning at 9 a.m. When Dave came into the CEO's office at the appointed time, I could tell he was agitated times ten. The heat coming off him was palpable, and I knew that if any word or gesture was even slightly misinterpreted, he was going to explode. Some 25 minutes later we were laughing. At that point, Dave said to us, "This morning I told my wife that she would likely see me before lunch today. I told her, 'They're giving me one of those evaluations, and if they say anything I don't like, I'm quitting.'" I'm glad it went well because Dave is still there and doing better than ever.

Developing employees who have been part of the organization for some time occasionally requires delicate handling. The most difficult part of the procedure is "history," as in previously misworded statements, arguments, misperceptions, and punishments that were not followed by "clean-up work," which I will discuss in detail in Chapter 5.

Generally speaking, history of this nature can cause a new manager to start at ground zero when dealing with a long-term employee. These negative dynamics must be overcome slowly; the manager can do this by presenting a new or different personal side. Any manager who wants to effectively develop a team must gain the trust of those employees. That takes time, so go slowly and ease into the MED Review. Remember to apply some of the same language covered at the beginning of Chapter 3.

The Manager and Employee Development Review: An 11-Step Process

The MED Review is built on the foundation of developing the skills of the manager as well as those of the employee. This must be a level playing field, because the employee will not accept a one-sided conversation directed at his or her faults while the manager rules with a seemingly perfect skill set. Who better to review the manager than the employee, just as the manager is in the best position to help the employee grow? This process creates the environment where honest teamwork can thrive, become strong, and survive.

The following is a step-by-step look at the MED Review:

Step 1: Three-day introduction. Introduce the MED Review process three days prior to the first scheduled meeting. If fewer days are provided, the participant does not have time to properly prepare; on the other hand, if given more than three days, the delay and resulting apprehension can cause undue stress that hurts more than it helps. It is best if the manager introduces the review with a conversational tone and an easygoing attitude. This will help to reduce unwarranted stress due to possibly negative past associations with the completely different and dreaded employee evaluations. Simply tell the employee that "we will be reviewing each other and it will be pleasant, like nothing you have experienced before." They won't believe you at first, which is why you must prove it during the actual review. This conversational tone will help them to reveal more during the next phase of the pre-assessment. Give them a copy of the pre-assessment and the actual review form. Explain that they will grade themselves and the manager will grade them on the same points, and then they will compare and discuss the respective grades. Once complete, the manager and the employee together outline areas for mutual improvement.

Step 2: Pre-assessment (step 1). Managers tell me that the biggest challenge with traditional employee evaluations comes from bringing up difficult topics that might hit a nerve, be incorrect, be worded poorly, or otherwise make the employee feel self-conscious. If a safe environment has been established, the employee will invite these discussions through the pre-assessment tool. The questions on this form are designed to prompt the employee to speak to their strengths as well as to areas in which they would like to make improvement. If they bring up these topics, they are in essence inviting a dialogue, which means that they trust the relationship enough to broach touchy topics. If they do not bring up obvious topics of concern, either trust has not been established or they are simply blind to their weaknesses. Most people are aware of their weaknesses because employers, significant others, and/or friends have brought them up before.

Step 3: Filling out the MED Review form. The first major benefit to the MED Review is that it will take the manager less than 10 minutes to complete it. This is a significant improvement over the usual 45–60 minutes or more that the average manager labors over a traditional employee evaluation. Familiar letter grades are used, and plusses and minuses are encouraged. This is a living document and worksheet, so making notes on the form is perfectly acceptable.

Step 4: Development is a two-way street. This process is called a manager *and* employee development review for a reason. The first time the manager and the employee engage in this review, it is recommended to schedule 60 minutes for the meeting due to the need to establish familiarity with the new process. Afterward, these meetings can easily be accomplished in less than 12 minutes. When the employee arrives, use a conversational tone and sit in such a way that there is *not* a table (or, at the minimum, only the corner of a table is) between you (see Figure 4.1). Sitting across from one another subconsciously creates an adversarial dynamic and will significantly reduce effectiveness. Once you are comfortably seated, first, have the employee read the pre-assessment and briefly discuss delicate topics that will be covered in more detail

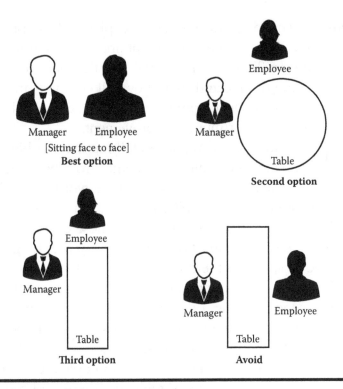

Figure 4.1   Optimal seating arrangement.

during the actual review. Second, go over areas of special interest to the employee and discuss how these may take place, along with the timing of these changes (i.e., now vs. six months from now). The main thing is to focus on what you can and will do, not hide behind the cloak of "we will see." That's a lie and the trust will be compromised from that point forward. The main objective of this process is to encourage and teach both the manager and the employee how to engage in honest dialogue toward mutual goals. Third, go over the grading procedure and move toward question one. Have the employee share his or her opinion of the grade first; only then should the manager offer a graded assessment. At this point a discussion should take place so that differences can be discussed and measured uniformly, and a compromise met. If this is a major area for improvement for either the employee or the manager, a star or other marking should be made on the document so that it can be addressed in the coaching and improvement stages. Fourth, the manager needs to ask how he or she can help the employee be more successful in each category. Conversation starters such as, "We both graded you a C+ in communication—how can I help or coach you to improve in that area?" are useful here. The employee will typically be hesitant to tell the supervisor what specific help is needed, so the manager must encourage the employee with statements such as, "What would be your best guess as to how I might be able to help you?" or "Might I run interference for you with other managers or people in their departments?" Remember, this is not a fishing expedition to find faults with others in the organization; rather, it is simply a way to help the employee and manager work more effectively with one another. Generally, after three or four questions, the mood and dynamic between the manager and the employee will soften and become more interactive. Continue to help one another find and discuss areas for improvement, remembering that the manager must have a strong-enough sense of self not to allow ego to ruin what is working. If the ego tries to rear its ugly head, the manager must make a note of it and get professional development. Otherwise, that manager's career will be stunted when he or she does this review in turn with a superior. In my experience, uncontrolled ego is the largest contributor of manager failure.

Step 5: Choosing joint development goals. As the manager and the employee have gone through the questions in the MED Review, they marked areas for mutual improvement. Now is the time to go back to those and prioritize them. Choose the top two or three depending on time and resources and write them down in the location provided.

Step 6: Finding the purpose. When establishing goals, consider how these activities will improve the department, the employee's performance, or the customer situation. If the joint development goals do not affect the internal or external customer in some direct way, then they are of no importance and you should choose a different goal. This section and the ensuing discussion between the manager and the employee help narrow down why a particular goal is worth pursuing.

Step 7: Identifying employee responsibilities. The employee is responsible for doing up to 80% of the work related to achieving the goals. These responsibilities need to be clearly outlined with timelines and measurement so that success can be properly monitored. It is best to measure something within one week, and then at regular intervals thereafter. These discussions do not have to be "formal." They can take place while passing in the hallway or at other times when the manager and the employee have two to three minutes to discuss and adjust. At least once per month, an "official" 10-minute meeting should take place to measure progress.

Step 8: Identifying manager responsibilities. As with the employee, the manager's responsibilities need to be written down and measured frequently. Is the manager training, coaching, and/or counseling? Is he or she providing the time necessary for the employee to complete his or her obligations? Is the manager improving and developing skills, or simply checking in with the employee? Remember, if an employee fails, much of that failure is directly attributed to poor management.

Step 9: Expected outcomes. Together, the manager and the employee should discuss and write down all expected outcomes. These might include goals such as the employee arriving to work 10 minutes early for 30 straight days; or the employee experiencing a 30% month-over-month improvement in accurate pick, pack, and shipping rate; or in the employee avoiding interruptions during meetings and instead providing solution-oriented, proactive, and helpful commentary.

Step 10: Actual outcomes. What are the actual outcomes being observed or measured? Are they in alignment with the expected outcomes? Are they better or worse? Make adjustments to encourage improvement. Remember that great teamwork requires development and discipline from both the manager and the employee. They are tied together in the success or failure of one another, and their superiors should be just as invested with their leader and manager development reviews.

Step 11: Follow-up schedule. Monitor at least one of these chosen goals after one week. This will reconnect the manager and the employee and start creating the necessary habits required for successful development. Then monitor results, at minimum, every 30 days thereafter. Once habits have been firmly established (generally after 90 days) and growth has been significantly measured by both parties, extend the official meetings out to a quarterly frequency.

Creating an Environment of Success

From the moment the employee walks into the office for the MED Review, it is up to the manager to choreograph how the process will unfold. I'm specifically referring here to the atmosphere in the room and feeling between the manager and the employee. Creating a casual yet professional environment is paramount to properly developing employees. If the employee feels reserved, fearful, or even angry, it is the manager's job to overcome these obstacles and create an environment of trust and true teamwork. If one of you fails, both fail, so it is paramount to stretch both you and the employee without causing stretch marks.

Consider the grading protocol in step 4 of the MED Review. Recall that the employee provides their grade first, followed by the manager expressing his or her opinion. A dialogue naturally follows, especially if there is a significant disparity between the two grades. In my experience, much of the difference may be related to interpretation, so it's imperative to define what each person is grading, and how. In my estimation, applying this single technique can help managers and employees overcome more than half of the misunderstandings that ever came between them. Because some review questions may be overly involved or present multiple dimensions of an employee's performance, feel free to break down and further define each one.

For example, in the category of "Commitment to Job," the language on which the employee will be graded states that he or she "Demonstrates a consistent, dependable work effort and positive work attitude."

In this example, it's quite possible that the employee may present with a very positive and enthusiastic work attitude but be sporadically undependable. If so, you may place a grade of "A" above the phrase "positive work attitude" and place a C+ above the phrase "dependable work effort." For the final grade, you would average all the grades and place it in the designated column (Figure 4.2).

Furthermore, you may decide that a "dependable work effort" is a very important part of the job in the case of a customer service rep, so this may be highlighted and added as a skill to be developed and placed on the development worksheet once the review is complete.

More on Setting and Reaching Goals

Once the graded question-and-answer portion of the MED Review is complete, both parties should look back over the review and choose the marked areas most in need of attention. Choose at least two but no more than five areas for improvement. The targeted areas must be difficult enough to stretch both people, but not so challenging that success is dubious. Three well-chosen areas for improvement are often about right, especially in the beginning when both the manager and the employee are learning this new process.

Employee

Manager & Employee Development Review
Employee

Name: John Doe ; Date: 10-19-16 ;
Department: Automotive ; Title: Team Leader ; Position Technician

Direct Supervisor: Joseph Doe Sr ; Title: Manager :

Definitions of Performance Ratings:

A - Excellent - Often exceeds all requirements of position
(Suggested development program outlined for additional responsibilities & possible advancement)

B – Very Capable – Performs above average in position.
(Suggested written coaching & development program outlined with regular follow-up in order to become an "A" player)

C - Satisfactory - Occasionally meets requirements of the position
(Written training, coaching and perhaps counseling, required to help this employee improve. Improvement program must be undertaken with follow-up reviews every month during the next six months)

D to F - Unsatisfactory - Fails to meet position requirements
(A last ditch effort must be made to transfer to a position better suited to their skills, or a decision must be made to either Train, Coach, Counsel or Terminate)

Category	Rating
1. **Volume of Work:** Maintains a steady & acceptable level of work:	C
a. Increases pace, if needed, so that deadlines can be met	A
b. Organizes work in order to obtain high productivity	D
Supporting example: *I understand the flow of work, I'm just not fast enough.*	
2. **Quality of Work:** Maintains acceptable standards of workmanship:	B
a. Completes work thoroughly without requiring constant correction	C
Supporting example: *I submit my work on time, but not complete.*	
3. **Job Knowledge:** Understands job procedures, equipment, methods, responsibilities and scope of work:	
a. Understands the operation (and limitations) of work	A
b. Keeps informed, makes use of proper standards & procedures	B
	C
Supporting example:	

+

Manager

Manager & Employee Development Review
Employee

Name: John Doe ; Date: 10-19-16 ;
Department: Automotive ; Title: Team Leader ; Position Technician

Direct Supervisor: Joseph Doe Sr ; Title: Manager :

Definitions of Performance Ratings:

A - Excellent - Often exceeds all requirements of position
(Suggested development program outlined for additional responsibilities & possible advancement)

B – Very Capable – Performs above average in position.
(Suggested written coaching & development program outlined with regular follow-up in order to become an "A" player)

C - Satisfactory - Occasionally meets requirements of the position
(Written training, coaching and perhaps counseling, required to help this employee improve. Improvement program must be undertaken with follow-up reviews every month during the next six months)

D to F - Unsatisfactory - Fails to meet position requirements
(A last ditch effort must be made to transfer to a position better suited to their skills, or a decision must be made to either Train, Coach, Counsel or Terminate)

Category	Rating
1. **Volume of Work:** Maintains a steady & acceptable level of work:	D
a. Increases pace, if needed, so that deadlines can be met	B
b. Organizes work in order to obtain high productivity	F
Supporting example: *Steady worker. No completed jobs yet. Not organized*	
2. **Quality of Work:** Maintains acceptable standards of workmanship:	B
a. Completes work thoroughly without requiring constant correction	C
Supporting example: *Continues to submit incomplete work.*	
3. **Job Knowledge:** Understands job procedures, equipment, methods, responsibilities and scope of work:	C
	B
a. Understands the operation (and limitations) of work	
b. Keeps informed, makes use of proper standards & procedures	A
Supporting example:	

=

A discussion between a manager and an employee on equal grounds.

Figure 4.2 Side by side development review.

To properly choose and achieve these goals, the manager and the employee must work together to understand the following four elements:

1. *Purpose.* If the area for improvement isn't tied directly to a larger issue, as seen in Figure 4.2, then it is of no value or is too insignificant to warrant your mutual attention. Do not skip this step because the conversations it creates are well worth the effort in deciding how this development will improve both the manager and the employee.
2. *Employee and manager responsibilities.* Let's think back to our SMART acronym mentioned in Chapter 2. The responsibilities for both the manager and the employee must be smart, measurable, attainable, relevant, and time-bound. As with this entire review process, it is invaluable to engage in dialogue during this time and develop these responsibilities together. Again, remember the ratio of 70:30. The employee is responsible for shouldering 70% of the load, while the manager is responsible for the remaining 30% related to training, coaching, and counseling the employee. In essence, it is the employee's job to do the heavy lifting in between meetings, while it is the manager's job to properly develop and hone his or her own training, coaching, and counseling skills.
3. *Expected outcomes.* This may take some work to fill in, but as with the other questions, it serves a vital purpose: it creates a visual target for the employee and the manager to shoot for, plus it is pivotal in planting the seed of a successful outcome within the minds of the participants. As I will share in Chapter 5, preparing the mind and implanting visual and auditory cues work like magic to create successful teams.
4. *Actual outcomes.* The last step in this procedure is to measure actual outcomes against target outcomes. If success is achieved, then it is wise to discuss how both of you were able to attain these results. The communication, behaviors, and discipline used to succeed can be easily transferred to subsequent development goals. If, however, the experimental coaching did not meet with success, then write down the answers to these questions:
   a. What went wrong?
   b. What went right?
   c. What changes need to be made to reduce the unsuccessful attempts and repeat more of the successful performances?
   d. When (specific date and time) will the measurement be revisited?

Refine this process until an acceptable amount of success is attained, always remembering that perfection is rarely an achievable goal. Sometimes

85% is good enough. Often pursuing "perfection" is a pipe dream, which just causes more problems between the manager and the employee. Be realistic and make good judgment calls regarding the quality of a given job or task.

The MED Review in Practice

Let's take a few moments to look at part of the "Joint Development Goals" portion of the MED Review form from the perspective of a manager, and complete it as if we were sitting down with an employee (Figure 4.3).
    Joint development goals:

■ Meet every Monday at 8 a.m. and prioritize objectives for the week.
■ Be careful of the language and tone you choose (no cursing or being mean-spirited to others).
■ Time cards of all your direct reports will be filled out and turned into Carol in accounting prior to 4:30 p.m. on the 1st and 15th of each month.

   Purpose: How will this activity improve the department, customer, or production (i.e., quality improvement, quantity improvement, target behavior expected, etc.)?

■ Meeting every Monday will help us keep the top priorities in front of us and aware of any changes. This will also help us improve our communication and teamwork.
■ Using profanity is unprofessional and very disrespectful to others. In addition, in this new age of business, swearing and other such behaviors are ripe for lawsuits and can be grounds for termination.
■ Timely submission of time cards is the process necessary so that everyone gets paid. In addition, Carol from accounting shouldn't have to track you or your people down pleading for time cards.

   Outline employee responsibilities (i.e., methods and actions):

■ Employee will come prepared to the Monday morning meeting, which means he will have to have this prepared by Friday afternoon or work on it over the weekend.

Manager

Joint Development Goals

1. *Meet every Monday at 8 a.m. and prioritize objectives for the week.*

2. *Be careful of the language and time you choose (no cursing or being mean spirited to others).*

3. *Time cards of all your direct reports will be filled out and turned into Carol in accounting prior to 4:50 p.m. on the 1st and 15th of each month.*

Purpose: How will this activity improve the department, customer or production: i.e., quality improvement, quantity improvement, target behavior expected etc.

1. *Meeting every Monday will help us keep the top priorities in front of us and aware of any changes. This will also help us improve our communication and teamwork.*

2. *Using profanity is unprofessional and very disrespectful to others. In addition, in this new age of business, swearing and other such behaviors are ripe for lawsuit and can be grounds for termination.*

3. *Timely submission of time cards is the process necessary so that everyone gets paid. On addition, Carol from accounting shouldn't have to track y/you or your people down pleading for time cards.*

Please outline **Employee** Responsibilities. i.e., methods and actions:
Employee will come prepared to the Monday morning meeting, which means he will have to have this prepared by Friday afternoon or work on it over the weekend.
Employee will be more aware of his speech while at work.
Employee will immediately apply methods taught and coached during our one-on-one meeting Monday morning.

Please outline **Supervisor** Responsibility. i.e., methods and actions:
Supervisor will come prepared to the Monday morning meetings, which means he will have to have this prepared by Friday afternoon or work on it over the weekend.
Supervisor will positively reinforce successful behavior.
Supervisor will coach employee on how to ensure that his direct reports fill out completed time and work projects on time card.

Please list **expected** outcome. **Be precise:**
Meeting are a top priority, and we will meet every Monday while both are in the building.
Cursing is eliminated and 100% success is attained.
Time cards will be thoroughly filled out, legible and turned in by 4:50 p.m. every 1st an 15th without exception.

Please list **actual** outcome and date for measurement evaluation. i.e., 30, 60, 90 days.

Employee signature: _____ . Date: _____

Supervisor signature: _____ . Date: _____

Overall comments from Supervisor:

Employee Remarks:

+

Employee

Joint Development Goals

1. *Meet every Monday at 8 a.m. and prioritize objective for the week.*

2. *Be careful of the language and time you choose (no cursing or being mean spirited to others).*

3. *Time cards of all your direct reports will be filled out and turned into Carol in accounting prior to 4:50 p.m. on the 1st and 15th of each month.*

Purpose: How will this activity improve the department, customer or production: i.e., quality improvement, quantity improvement, target behavior expected etc.

1. *Meeting every Monday will help us keep the top priorities in front of us and aware of any changes. This will also help us improve our communication and teamwork.*

2. *Using profanity is unprofessional and very disrespectful to others. In addition, in this new age of business, swearing and other such behaviors are ripe for lawsuit and can be grounds for termination.*

3. *Timely submission of time cards is the process necessary so that everyone gets paid. On addition, Carol from accounting shouldn't have to track y/you or your people down pleading for time cards.*

Please outline **Employee** Responsibilities. i.e., methods and actions:
Employee will come prepared to the Monday morning meeting, which means he will have to have this prepared by Friday afternoon or work on it over the weekend.
Employee will be more aware of his speech while at work.
Employee will immediately apply methods taught and coached during our one-on-one meeting Monday morning.

Please outline **Supervisor** Responsibility. i.e., methods and actions:
Supervisor will come prepared to the Monday morning meetings, which means he will have to have this prepared by Friday afternoon or work on it over the weekend.
Supervisor will positively reinforce successful behavior.
Supervisor will coach employee on how to ensure that his direct reports fill out completed time and work projects on time card.

Please list **expected** outcome. **Be precise:**
Meeting are a top priority, and we will meet every Monday while both are in the building.
Cursing is eliminated and 100% success is attained.
Time cards will be thoroughly filled out, legible and turned in by 4:50 p.m. every 1st an 15th without exception.

Please list **actual** outcome and date for measurement evaluation. i.e., 30, 60, 90 days.

Employee signature: _____ . Date: _____

Supervisor signature: _____ . Date: _____

Overall comments from Supervisor:

Employee Remarks:

= A joint discussion between a manager and an employee on equal grounds.

Figure 4.3 Joint development goals.

- Employee will be more aware of his speech while at work.
- Employee will immediately apply methods taught and coached during our one-on-one meeting Monday morning.

Outline supervisor responsibility (i.e., methods and actions):

- Supervisor will come prepared to the Monday morning meetings, which means he or she must have this prepared by Friday afternoon or work on it over the weekend.
- Supervisor will positively reinforce successful behavior.
- Supervisor will coach employee on how to ensure that his or her direct reports fill out completed time and work projects on time card.

Precisely list expected outcomes:

- Meetings are a top priority, and we will meet every Monday while both are in the building.
- Cursing is eliminated and 100% success is attained.
- Time cards will be thoroughly filled out, legible, and turned in by 4:30 every 1st and 15th without exception.

List actual outcome and date for measurement evaluation (i.e., 30, 60, 90 days):

- All three of these objectives will be measured at 30-day intervals for the next 90 days (Figure 4.4).

Casual in-the-Hall Meetings

As both the manager and the employee become more successful at communicating, developing trust, and making changes in their behaviors, they will graduate to informal meetings that may take place in casual locations such as hallways. I suggest you stay on a structure for at least the first 90 days, and thereafter you can start in the hall meetings. However, these must take place on a very frequent basis or much of the ground made during the first 90 days will be lost. Once the manager and the employee learn how successful they can be through weekly "huddles," that success in and of itself becomes self-reinforcing, because everyone loves to be part of a winning team. Winning teams communicate clearly and frequently (think how

Step 1: Self-Development

Self-Development Inquiry
Part One of the Manager & Employee Development Review Process

1. Take an objective look at your working, management, or leadership style and skills during the past 6-12 months. **Part One:** Please list 2-3 strengths and/or personal characteristics which have helped you excel or be productive as an employee, manager, or leader. **Part Two:** Please list 2-3 limitations that continue to impede your progress as an effective employee, manager or leader.

2. Please outline 3-5 areas as an employee, manager or leader where you would like additional training, coaching and supportive Professional Development. How might these improved skills, business insights, and industry knowledge improve the customer experience? Improve your department and/or company? And advance your personal and professional value as an employee, manager or leader?

Step 2: Development Review

Manager & Employee Development Review
Employee

Name: _____ ;Date: _____ ;
Department: _____ ;Title: _____ ; Position _____ ;

Direct Supervisor: _____ ; Title: _____ ;

Definitions of Performance Ratings:

A - Excellent - Often exceeds all requirements of position
(Suggested development program outlined for additional responsibilities & possible advancement)

B – Very Capable – Performs above average in position.
(Suggested written coaching & development program outlined with regular follow-up in order to become an "A" player)

C - Satisfactory - Occasionally meets requirements of the position
(Written training, coaching and perhaps counseling, required to help this employee improve. Improvement program must be undertaken with follow-up reviews every month during the next six months)

D to F - Unsatisfactory - Fails to meet position requirements
(A last ditch effort must be made to transfer to a position better suited to their skills, or a decision must be made to either Train, Coach, Counsel or Terminate)

Category	Rating
1. **Volume of Work:** Maintains a steady & acceptable level of work:	_____
a. Increases pace, if needed, so that deadlines can be met	_____
b. Organizes work in order to obtain high productivity	_____
Supporting example: _____	
2. **Quality of Work:** Maintains acceptable standards of workmanship:	_____
a. Completes work thoroughly without requiring constant correction	_____
Supporting example: _____	
3. **Job Knowledge:** Understands job procedures, equipment, methods, responsibilities and scope of work:	
a. Understands the operation (and limitations) of work	_____
b. Keeps informed, makes use of proper standards & procedures	_____
Supporting example: _____	

4. **Commitment to Job:** Demonstrates a consistent, dependable work effort and positive work attitude.	
a. Is flexible; Adapts easily to changes in work assignments	_____
b. Is eager to take on additional responsibilities	_____
Supporting example: _____	
5. **Attendance and Punctuality:** Uses company time properly	
a. Arrives and leaves at proper time, uses breaks appropriately	_____
b. Gives proper advance notice in case of absence.	_____
Supporting example: _____	
6. **Safety and Maintenance:** Ensures safety of self & others through proper use and care of equipment/work site.	
a. Handles & operates equipment in a careful manner	_____
b. Stores and maintains equipment properly & communicates maintenance issues to proper supervisor according to protocol.	_____
Supporting example: _____	
7. **Communicates Information:** Communicates ideas & information in a clear, concise and timely manner	
a. Provides complete, reliable and prompt information to supervisor and co-workers.	
b. Keeps accurate records of completed work and appropriate documents/work orders.	_____
Supporting example: _____	
8. **Cooperation:** Works with others to do a good job for the day and week.	
a. Functions well as a team member, gets along with fellow employees	_____
b. Follows instruction; accepts work assignments willingly	_____
Supporting example: _____	

Figure 4.4   Steps 1 and 2. Self-development and MED Review. Complete full-sized examples in Appendix.

unsuccessful football teams would be if they didn't adhere to these basic building blocks of communication during an entire game). The main thing to ensure while doing in the hall meetings is confidentiality, so be careful that others cannot overhear if the topic is of a private matter.

Now that we have gone over what to do during a successful MED Review and how to go about it, in Chapter 5 I will share with you the psychological underpinnings of this process.

Summary

Successful managers at winning organizations understand the value generated by employees who take the time to fully interact with and understand one another. Effective communication skills, therefore, are foundational in building successful business relationships. Effective communication doesn't just happen, however. It is a learned skill that needs continuous updating and refinement, and great managers will encourage, nurture, and reward this behavior in their direct reports. This takes desire, discipline, practice, and consistent effort over time so that it becomes a habit.

Four Barriers to Good Communication

1. *Mind reading.* Never assume you know what the other person is thinking. Ask. Be specific.
2. *Storing up annoyances and grievances.* It is better to express minor annoyances or concerns as they occur rather than store and "dump" them all at once.
3. *Withholding relevant negative information.* Successful managers solve problems in the fastest and least disruptive way. The quicker a problem is "on the table," the quicker it can be resolved, and the quicker everyone can return to being productive.
4. *Using put-downs, certain kinds of humor and other disrespectful behaviors.* In arguments or disagreements, stick to the point. In every interaction, there are two messages. The first and most obvious message is the content itself. These are the facts, goals, and topic at hand. The second and more powerful message is the way in which the content is delivered. "It's not what you say, but how you say it," or "Think before you speak." These may be old sayings, but they remain in use for a good reason: they're relevant.

Seven Ways to Improve Communication

1. Keep your messages clear and consistent.
2. Use the other person's words, metaphors, and analogies.
3. Pay attention and listen carefully.
4. Develop trust.
5. Let people know that you understand their point of view.

6. Speak for yourself. You can do this by using "I" statements rather than "you" statements.
7. Don't hog. Let other people have their say. I will go one step further and advise you to encourage other people to express their opinions or ideas.

The MED Review: An 11-Step Process

The MED Review is built on the foundation of developing the skills of the manager as well as those of the employee. This must be a level playing field, because the employee will not accept a one-sided conversation directed at his or her faults while the manager rules with a seemingly perfect skill set. Who better to review the manager than the employee, just as the manager is in the best position to help the employee grow? This process creates the environment where honest teamwork can thrive, become strong, and survive.

Step 1: Three-day introduction. Introduce the MED Review process three days prior to the first scheduled meeting.

Step 2: Pre-assessment (step 1). If a safe environment has been established, the employee will invite difficult discussions through the pre-assessment tool.

Step 3: Filling out the MED Review form. The first major benefit to the MED Review is that it will take the manager less than 10 minutes to complete it.

Step 4: Development is a two-way street. When the employee arrives, use a conversational tone and sit in such a way that there is *not* a table (or, at the minimum, only the corner of a table is) between you.

Step 5: Choosing joint development goals. Choose the top two or three depending on time and resources and write them down in the location provided.

Step 6: Finding the purpose. When establishing goals, consider how these activities will improve the department, the employee's performance, or the customer situation.

Step 7: Identifying employee responsibilities. The employee is responsible for doing up to 80% of the work related to achieving the goals. It is best to measure something within one week, and then at regular intervals thereafter.

Step 8: Identifying manager responsibilities. As with the employee, the manager's responsibilities need to be written down and measured frequently. Remember, if an employee fails, much of that failure is directly attributed to poor management.

Step 9: Expected outcomes. Together, the manager and the employee should discuss and write down all expected outcomes.

Step 10: Actual outcomes. What are the actual outcomes being observed or measured? Are they in alignment with the expected outcomes? Remember that great teamwork requires development and discipline from both the manager and the employee.

Step 11: Follow-up schedule. Monitor at least one of these chosen goals after one week. This will reconnect the manager and the employee and start creating the necessary habits required for successful development.

Chapter 5

Where Evolved Mindsets Lead, Transformative Teamwork Follows

To achieve greatness, one must first think greatness.

Kelly Graves

Following Up after the Review with the Evolved Mindset

When Darwin first made famous the term "survival of the fittest," I do not believe he was talking about the strongest species or the fastest but rather those species most able to adapt quickly to changing surroundings. Welcome to the early part of the twenty-first century where technology has morphed into something one could not imagine just 50 years ago. However, as miraculous as technology has grown, human communication has stagnated. Sure, our communication between people has become quicker, but it is more superficial than ever, but this is where those able to adapt to ever increasing knowledge bridging the gap between business and psychology will evolve to a level of success unequaled. In essence, what I am about to share with you regarding communication and development is equivalent to the microchip processor in the 1960s. In Chapter 4, we discussed how to go about choreographing the manager and employee review. In this chapter, we will be discussing how to prepare and lead one's mind toward success in an evolutionary way.

What you feed your mind and what you feed the employees mind is of enormous consequence because subtle changes in wording can have profound effects on mental health and subsequent behavior. As I mentioned above, to achieve greatness, one must first think greatness and thinking greatness is motivated by belief.

Beliefs form through a combination of experience, environment, and the meaning we make out of both. As managers, one can help shape an employee's perception and thinking about their experiences and the messages received from the environment, and the impact of his/her belief in the possibilities that exist through their commitment and hard work. Beliefs can be changed through experiences and authority figures that challenge an existing mindset in a supportive setting. In essence, one's beliefs about one's abilities to expand are flexible by shifting their thoughts or mindsets.

Toward a New Way of Thinking and Managing

Mindset can be defined as a view employees have of their successes, mistakes, fears, and triumphs and plays a pivotal role in an individual's capacity to learn and change. In *Mindset: The New Psychology of Success*, Stanford University researcher Carol Dweck writes that mindsets are powerful drivers of perceptions about self and others as well as one's capabilities and place in the world. They guide the whole interpretation process. Dweck's work identifies two distinctly different mindsets that have the greatest implications for successful learning and change over the lifespan: the "Fixed Mindset" and the "Growth Mindset."

"A growth mindset is when you believe that through your own efforts you can cultivate your personal qualities. If you have this belief, then you are more likely to have a passion for learning because you believe you are developing your qualities. Also, rather than seeing a challenge as something to avoid because it will reveal your weaknesses, you welcome it because you see it as an opportunity to grow and learn" (Dweck 2008).

A fixed mindset, on the other hand, is when one believes human qualities are carved in stone. If you feel "you only have a certain amount of intelligence a certain personality, and a certain moral character, then all you can do is prove that you have the traits you have and hide your deficiencies" (Dweck 2008).

In a growth mindset, you do not always welcome setbacks, but you understand that it is information on how to move forward better next time. In a fixed mindset, a setback calls your ability into question. Everything is about: Am I smart? Am I not smart? However, if you are always managing your image to look sharp, you are not focusing on stretching your boundaries, you are not thinking about them in the most constructive ways, and you are not sticking to things that don't work right away (Figure 5.1).

Whether we are praising or criticizing, Dweck "suggests that you focus on the process, not on the person." So, if there is a success, even a great achievement, you do not say, "you are a superstar" or that "you have natural talent" because it puts people into a fixed mindset. Thus, it makes them afraid of doing hard things or of making mistakes, which will dampen future creativity or innovation. If, however, "you are giving negative feedback, it should be about the process rather than the person. So, you can praise what was good about the process, but then you can also analyze what was wrong with the process and what the person can do to increase the likelihood of succeeding next time" (Glei n.d.). Here are some examples of a manager providing feedback.

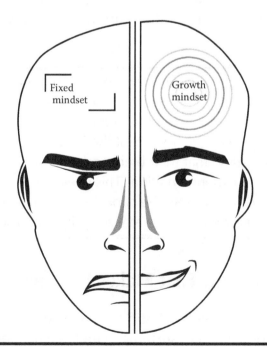

Figure 5.1   Fixed and growth mindset.

A fixed-mindset approach would be saying something like

> This project turned out just the way we intended. You are a super-star. I knew you had the natural ability and this is proof of it.

as opposed to a growth-mindset approach of

> John this project turned out very well. I appreciated the way you brought the team together, kept everyone focused, and created a sense of ownership.

Here are examples of providing constructive criticism.

When a manager is giving criticism, you need to critique the process someone engaged in and discuss what skills he or she needs to learn and improve.

Dweck says to use the word—"yet." You can say to someone who fell short: "You do not seem to have this," but then add the word "yet." As in, "You do not seem to have these skills…yet." By doing that, we give people a time perspective. It creates the idea of learning over time. It puts the other person on that learning curve and says, "Well, maybe you are not at the finish line, but you are on that learning curve and let's go further" (Glei n.d.).

Brain plasticity: Cutting edge research shows that we can grow our brain and increase our intelligence over the lifespan. The essence of the "growth" mind-set knows the way our brains expand through new experiences, challenges, and tasks. Many people struggle to accept the idea that they can change, and it helps them to understand that their brain seeks out and gets excited by novelty, inventiveness, and experimentation. This goes to the heart of what therapists and counselors do—promote the capacity to change and grow, and help clients develop the skills they need to realize their goals (Merzenich 2009).

It's Effort, Not Talent, That Makes Employees Successful

A recent series of studies led by Heslin (2005), who leads the EMBA Managerial Skills course at the Australian Graduate School of Management, considered the implications of fixed mindsets and how they can be changed. It turns out that managers with a fixed mindset tend to demoralize everyone, including themselves. Also, his research delved deeper into employee reactions including demoralization, disengagement, absenteeism, and turnover, and a sense that they are not being given a fair go by their manager.

"It is imperative to recognize how readily a vicious cycle can be created by anchoring on a negative first impression of someone's performance capabilities," he says. "A person's initial achievements in a role are often not predictive of what they are ultimately able to achieve. Employees resent feeling unsupported and underestimated. Imagine how frustrating it would be to be managed by someone who did not believe in your potential to improve your performance or advance in your career" (Business Strategy 2012).

"Managers with a fixed mindset can also be dysfunctional in how they deal with top performers," Heslin says. After categorizing someone as a star, a fixed mindset can lead managers not to recognize when remedial action is needed.

In a series of studies published in 2005, a collaboration among Heslin, Gary Latham from the University of Toronto, and Don VandeWalle of Southern Methodist University found that "a fixed mindset blinded managers to variation above or below an employee's initial performance level. On the other hand, those with a growth mindset were more data-driven, less anchored by past impressions, and therefore more capable of providing an accurate and unbiased appraisal of employee performance" (Business Strategy 2012).

Subsequent research by Heslin and his colleagues found that "employees believed managers with a growth mindset were more willing and capable of providing helpful on-the-job coaching." It makes sense that if fixed-mindset managers were skeptical about employees' ability to change, they would be unlikely to invest time and resources in coaching their employees.

Heslin's latest work, again coauthored with VandeWalle and published in the *Journal of Management*, sheds initial light on how employees react to managers as a function of managers' mindsets. In short, "it shows that when managers hold a growth mindset, employees feel that they receive a more procedurally fair performance appraisal (probably reflecting it being more data-based, accurate and supplemented with coaching). Employees will thus be more committed and willing to go the extra mile for their organization" (Business Strategy 2012).

Organizationally Driven Growth Mindset

When questioning what organizations can do to create a culture that leads people to a growth mindset, again we look to the research conducted by Peter Heslin and colleagues (2006). They looked at managers with a growth mindset and managers with a fixed mindset. They found that managers with a growth mindset were more open to feedback and criticism from subordinates than managers with a fixed mindset. Managers with a growth mindset believe not only in their growth but also in the growth of other people. The findings also show that growth-minded managers notify changes in skills and functioning of subordinates, instead of fixed-minded managers who stick to their first impressions of subordinates. They do not notify development of their subordinates, who are consequently not rewarded for their growth. Furthermore, their research shows that managers with a growth mindset provide better coaching than fixed-minded managers. This is of no surprise since fixed-minded managers believe that people's capabilities are fixed, so why coach them if that will not help? Briefly summarized, managers with a growth mindset encourage and recognize the growth of subordinate's abilities.

It is helpful to educate managers about the whole idea of mindsets and encourage them to develop a growth mindset. It is essential that, having developed managers, the work environment is more growth-minded, accomplished with the manager and employee review. Growth-mindset managers naturally apply growth-minded organizational practices, and organizational policies should be aligned to that. How can an individual start to change his or her mindset?

As a first step, Dweck says to start listening to the fixed-mindset voice in your head. It is always there telling you, "Oh, are you sure you want to do this? You might make mistakes and, you know, people will find you out. You are not going to look like the genius you want to look like." If you start struggling, the fixed mindset says, "Oh, I told you so, but it is not too late; you can still get out and save face." For a while just do that, just start listening to the fixed-mindset voice keeping score. "And then over time: Start talking back. Do it most of all if you still feel threatened, because we all have a little part of ourselves that is a little shy, a little threatened. Do it anyway! Moreover, see how well it works" (Business Strategy 2012).

Applying the Growth Mindset

Now let's bring this down to practical terms by using a growth mindset while developing employees using Allan Weiss' four steps of developing employees (Weiss 2000, pp. 80–84). These are

1. We *train* employees.
2. We *coach* employees. Moreover, hopefully, this is where it stops!
3. When employees have personal problems laced with emotional issues, we do our best to help *counsel* them back to health. When done effectively, they move back into the training and coaching model of development.
4. If managers have done their best at training, coaching, and counseling the employee, then it is both a relief and healthier for the employee and the organization to part company. Therefore, the last stage is *termination*.

Training

"We are most familiar with training. We use it to teach new skills, convey information relevant to the organization, meet federal regulations, and enhance technical proficiency. Training is also the first thing we think of when there is a problem to be addressed or an organizational change to be presented" (Weiss 2000, pp. 80–84).

In Chapter 3, I wrote about developing a new employee from day one. It is best to follow this same pattern with a new employee and periodically with long-term employees. Improved training methods, whether that be skill set or customer service training, should be planned for during the yearly organizational and department strategic planning meetings.

In my experience, training programs are either not done, done poorly, or done haphazardly when time allows. We know there is rarely enough time in the day to achieve what's already on the to-do list, so if you are looking for "free time" it will never materialize on its own. One must make time for training and development and schedule it in. Below are some suggestions:

Create a minimum of a two-hour training course for all employees that you implement every month or two when new employees have been hired on. In smaller companies where growth is not as quick, or turnover is not an issue, one can do them when a new person is hired. Here is what we did at AM, Inc.

Once the executive team was finished going through the vision, mission, core values, team building exercise, communication and trust building, and team development plan, Brandon and Leif created a new employee on-boarding session teaching these same traits. We blended new employees and started working our way through all current employees at about fifteen people in each group. Then we divided them into two smaller groups so people would speak up and get involved and this approach worked out quite well.

Group facilitation suggestion: if you keep the group size between five and eight, people will tend to speak up and talk back and forth much better than you would get in higher numbered groups. So, the lesson is, create smaller groups and meet more frequently and get significantly more accomplished. It is imperative to be proactive with how you would like the grapevine to function.

It is a matter of human instinct that people will gossip and share information. I have never read of a psychological technique that stops the gossip, so if we cannot stop it, then the least we can do is introduce some content in a proactive manner. If management has done a good job developing their employees and creating an environment of trust and communication, the grapevine should be fairly easy to tame. The key is in being proactive.

Once one comes to terms that the grapevine is real and humming along nicely, the next logical step is to say we want to develop and grow a healthy company, so how can we feed the grapevine fresh honest content that embodies our company message? The technique is to get closer to your people and admit your humanness, that part of you that does not always do everything perfectly. By modeling that,

1. Management does their best, but they do not always get along so they must practice the same techniques they are teaching and coaching their employees. Moreover, even though they have done it and coached it hundreds of times, it can still make them anxious and a little fearful, but these feelings are very normal. It is OK to be anxious *and* take the step into the unknown anyway. That is what our forefathers called courage. Winston Churchill said, "failure is seldom fatal, and success never final—it is courage that counts."

2. They plan and prepare and still make mistakes, Yes! Admit that management makes mistakes, quit lying to your employees, they talk and know when mistakes happen and what makes it worse is when you browbeat them for making a ten-dollar error, and they know management recently made a ten-thousand-dollar mistake. This type of behavior enrages people so cop to it and learn together. Bring it up for discussion in a logical way so that confidentiality is maintained, and those who made the mistakes are held in safe regard or even touted as being courageous enough to attempt the feat now what we can learn from it and move on without people getting in trouble.

Success Evolves by Involving Your Employees (Graves 2016a)

Go back to basics by involving your people—in other words, ask them. A few years ago I participated in a company merger. Company A had purchased company B, and many of the company B people were going to be laid off within the following twelve months. My job was to help the managers motivate themselves as well as the employees in company B while continuing to maintain production levels and delivery schedules.

I started off by respecting people and listening to their fears, concerns, and frustrations. The next step was to outline a realistic production plan that everyone could support, given the dire situation. The last step was to find and maintain a healthy balance between these two worlds. I held meetings with small groups of around seven to eight people and asked them their ideas on how to go about this transition. Slowly the conversations turned from venting to finding solutions to the challenges that faced us all. I had my training and experience on how to move through this transition in an efficient and effective manner; the managers had their ideas on the subject, and the employees had their thoughts as well. The key was to gather all of this information and use bits and pieces from each individual or group so that a hybrid was created. I knew things they did not, the managers knew things the employees did not, but the employees knew things that neither the mangers nor I knew about. In the end, the transition went as smoothly as it could have, and we were successful by gathering valuable input from everyone; but more importantly we gained support and buy-in from everyone involved. If respect had not been provided, questions asked, and answers honestly heard and acknowledged, people might have fought this painful transition at every turn and may have even consciously or unconsciously sabotaged the process out of anger, frustration, and loss.

During challenging times, leaders often assume they must have all the answers or think they do not have a chance to get input and quickly implement. What is needed, at moments like these more than ever, is to connect with your people and involve them. The answers you seek are housed within the human talent that you have cultivated over the years. Your job as a manager is to encourage them to share this point of view with you and for you to *listen*. Employees have a point of view that you cannot because of their position. Many of your employees know the customer and the needs of the customer better than you because they communicate with the customer every day and are not stuck behind your desk crunching numbers or stuck in meetings with politicians. They often know how to improve the processes, where cost savings can come from—yes, even the severe cost savings measures.

Coaching

"Coaching is both proactive and reactive support provided to employees to improve their performance and help them when having difficulties. It is mainly focused on maintaining existing, strong performance and improving it still further" (Weiss 2000, pp. 80–84).

All employees should be coached on an ongoing basis. It is a form of mentoring or advising that enables ongoing dialogue between the manager and the employee so that feedback on performance does not occur only when there is a problem. Moreover, it allows for excellent work to be recognized, supported, exploited, and conveyed to others.

Consequently, good managers spend ten times more of their efforts and energy on coaching than on counseling. Poor managers confuse the two, don't understand the difference, and usually respond only to problems, meaning that a significant amount of their time is spent on correcting weaknesses rather than on supporting strengths.

Coaching focuses on short-term objectives, to develop specific skills or behaviors by improving what already exists.

Coaching should be part of a manager's daily schedule.

- It can be both proactive and reactive.
- It can involve supporting and mentoring.

■ It is provided to employees to improve their performance.
■ It is focused on maintaining existing strong performance and improving it still further.

1. Once a year, the manager and the employee create a development plan that includes areas of continued growth and gratification for the employee as well as areas that add contributions to the organization (not remedial areas).
2. The manager and the employee agree on specific actions required of both to meet the goals.
3. The manager and the employee meet formally once a month or quarter, depending on circumstances, to review progress and modify the plan as needed.
4. The manager builds into his or her weekly calendar and priorities time for each person in the coaching relationship. This may be 5–10 minutes to review progress on a project or an hour spent on a new technique being implemented. These should not be formal meetings, but rather give and take while the manager and the employee help to coach one another.
5. The manager also makes it a practice to spontaneously spend a few minutes with employees as conditions merit, praising a consistent and determined work ethic, inquiring if help is needed with a difficult situation or customer, or offering a new perspective.

■ The dialogue is constant and ongoing, not oriented around a periodic review.
■ The feedback is timely, offered at a point where an issue, performance, or problem arises.
■ The manager advises, but the employee performs.
■ Coaching is overwhelmingly positively oriented or neutral. The manager does provide negative feedback when there is clear evidence that the employee's judgment was wrong, actions were inappropriate, or performance was below standards.
■ The manager is approachable; the employee feels comfortable initiating conversations and requesting feedback.
■ Employees become coaches themselves to subordinates and peers.

When coaching: A leader's main job is to awaken the genius within his or her people. Stoke the fires of hope, stoke the fires of vision, and stoke the fires of a growth mindset: in other words, of what some could be. To believe in your employees so much they believe it themselves, which becomes a self-fulfilling prophecy (Figure 5.2).

■ Think of what a child does to walk or talk. They mimic the behavior they see. Parents hold their hands and support them; parents let them take risks and walk from the couch to the coffee table, and good parents let them fall and struggle, but with loving encouragement. The concept is the same with employees. Human nature is very essential. We learn by watching and learning from others; we learn by people telling us what we are doing right and not by scolding us. There are times when pain or negative reinforcement is required, but that is the last resort when all other options have been exhausted, and I will explain the steps to that in a later section of this chapter. Managers who rely too quickly on pain, fear, and ridicule are lazy, weak, and ignorant managers who are not smart enough to educate themselves about human nature (which is why you are reading this book; congratulations for taking steps to educate yourself and gain new knowledge). They are simply a hammer seeing employees and problems as nails to hit. In this

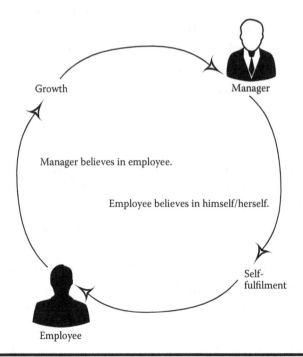

Figure 5.2 Belief system.

day and age, it is inexcusable to be that type of a manager or to have such a blunt instrument working for you and in charge of others. It says a lot about the CEO. He/she does not have his/her finger on the pulse of his/her organization and doesn't know any other methods as well. In other words, our technology is light years ahead of 90% of the manager's employee development skills.

■ Instead of telling employees to do a task, try this "leading" technique instead. Ask the employee what might happen if you did this differently; when they answer, ask them what might be the first step, then the second step, and what might be the toughest part of it and how you might overcome that obstacle. By using this "leading" method, the employees develop the plan themselves with your guidance. The only difference is once they have developed their program, in their words, and thought it through or visualized it in their unique way, they will be able to execute on it because they understand it. That is the essence of coaching. Remember this:

  – If we tell an employee, they will *not* understand.
  – If we show an employee, they *may* understand.
  – If we involve an employee, they *will* understand and follow through.
  – Each week gives them a new challenge or problem to solve using this coaching method. Once you have taken them through these steps, eight to ten times they will be able to do most of it on their own and teach others the same technique.
  – When the challenges get bigger, and the risks higher, employees will come to you since their confidence to handle the major issues may not be sufficient. Again, don't give them the answer; ask them and solve it together. This coaching method will teach them step by step your thought and decision-making process. When they do make a mistake, which they undoubtedly will, you do not scold but rather reinforce the attempt and hard work and then ask them to take you through the thought process step by step. In this way, you can help them improve in the single area where they made a mistake. Perhaps it was not a mistake. Perhaps their logic paralleled yours, but they cut a corner and dropped the ball, so they improved at seven of the eight steps so reinforce those seven successes. The main point to remember is that coaching is about guiding and shaping with a growth mindset. That is how the mind best functions and learns.
  – When encouraging employees, reinforce their work ethic and effort, not their ability. Remember, Dweck's research has shown that when parents and employers reinforced ability, the person spiked quickly

due to the attention but then dropped to lower levels because the praise was focused on their ability that they saw as having or not having. When subsequent challenges came, their ability alone did not serve them, and they spiraled. Conversely, those people who were praised for the work ethic and effort improved with every new task and challenge because the effort was being measured. All successful people know this intuitively. For the most part, it is your effort that has propelled you, not your ability alone. Ask any coach who will go further: the player with natural ability or the player with stamina to keep going after hitting the wall.

It Is Virtually Impossible to Have Happy External Customers If You Have Unhappy Internal Customers

The brutal truth is this: It is virtually impossible to have happy external customers when you have unhappy internal customers, i.e., employees! Every point of contact made by an unhappy employee will negatively impact the external customer relationship. Even when employees do their very best to hide their displeasure, it comes across through voice inflection, what they say and what they do not, how hard they work to please the customer or to produce a better product or deliver a quality service. These thoughts, actions, and behaviors can be unknown to the employee but they inadvertently surface; how can they not if the employee feels slighted or taken advantage of?

Internal customers are people who make up the other departments that work inside your business. For example, accounting, sales, engineering, production, finance, and marketing are each other's customers. For your organization to function smoothly and profitably, people within and between departments must communicate clearly, organize tasks and timelines, and implement in an effective and efficient manner.

The more effective people are at serving one another, the smoother their processes will be, and they will achieve better results in production, innovation, sales, efficiencies, and profits.

Here are suggestions on how to provide stellar internal customer service:

1. Be aware of what you think about yourself and how you coach your employees. Behavior follows thought. Are your thoughts helping you and building you and your employees up, or are your thoughts hurting you or your employees, and making circumstances more difficult

between you? Practice a growth mindset and respectful thoughts will follow.

2. Communicate clearly and often when coaching. Ask for clarification when you are unsure of what is conveyed through verbal and nonverbal means.

3. Talk face-to-face or by phone instead of using e-mail. The benefits of this process far outweigh the time saved by using e-mail. Too much e-mail can be a crutch and severely impact the communication between a manager and an employee working to achieve common goals.

4. Conduct department-to-department development meetings so that people can ask each other for information, clarification, and process refinement. I call this "speed dating" for departments. Gather staff from each department and give those people 10–15 minutes to ask people from another department for what they need or could provide to make their processes function more smoothly. In other words, sales need more precise delivery schedules from production so they can do JIT deliveries with customers. Conversely, what do the production people need from sales to make their jobs easier, more productive, efficient, and fun? Prioritize these ideas, assign who will do what by when, and then monitor in 30 days to determine results and make adjustments. In fewer than 60 minutes, people in both departments will have gathered tons of precise information about how to be better customers to one another and, as a result, deliver better products and services to the external customer. Plus, each group will have created a better understanding of the other and formed a new appreciation for what their colleagues do and how much they already help one another.

5. Talk about the pink elephant in the corner that everyone knows about and talks about in his or her "cliques" but doesn't address directly in formal meetings. These "taboo" topics are the core problems that cripple organizations. When colleagues learn to work through their misunderstandings and collaborate, they will be in a strong position to significantly increase production, performance, and profits.

Counseling: "Counseling is the reactive, structured approach implemented when an employee is performing below expectations, due to either a skill deficiency or an attitude deficiency. It is mainly focused on restoring performance to a minimally acceptable level or, failing that, removing the employee from that job" (Weiss 2000, pp. 80–84).

Use a structured counseling approach when an employee is performing below expectations due to either a skill deficit or attitude deficit. Have a counseling conversation as soon as possible at the moment when a performance deviation becomes apparent.

- Check to see if there are obstacles to desired performance—barriers that would inhibit even a skilled and motivated worker.
- The manager must be prepared.
- Determine if the poor performance is caused by skills deficit or poor attitude.
- Focus on the behavior and the evidence.
- Obtain agreement on the standard and the actual performance in question.
- Discuss the impact of the performance on others in the organization.
- Consider the manager's available alternatives and the consequences for the employee.
- Establish an action plan for improvement with dates and accountability.
- Review and monitor progress.
- Make a decision.

Counseling 101 and the 3-Day Rule

In general, people hate confrontation and will do just about anything to distance themselves from it, but a manager owes it to his or her employees to overcome this fear and do what's right. The key is knowing how to handle it and knowing what will happen before it happens, and in doing so, one can be prepared ahead of time and not surprised.

Sally, the owner of DS Inc., told me she wanted to terminate an employee, Marg. I told her that she had to try something first. She had to sit with Marg and be truthful about what she was doing wrong.

1. Sally said she was not sure she could tell that to Marg's face.
2. She was fearful of the confrontation. I told her:

She owed it to Marg, to be honest, and counsel her because she had nothing to lose since she was planning on terminating Marg anyway, so let's use this opportunity as "practice." Using this technique helps take the sting out of being real since a "practice run" is often mired in mistakes, so I was encouraging her to forget about mistakes and just go through with the counseling. Also, I told her I would walk her through the process of being empathetic yet firm while practicing mindful counseling skills.

The next day at 10 a.m., Sally called Marg into her office and invited her to sit at the corner of her desk so they would form a semicircle rather than be face to face with a table in between them.

Sally mentioned that she had gone through various forms of training and coaching over the last seven months, but Marg did not seem to get the hang of the procedures the other employees at DS adhered to. Marg started to defend herself, but it was time for Sally to take charge and lead, and again she encouraged Marg to listen for now and assured her that she would get her turn shortly. Sally began again with outlining what was expected of her, being very clear to list behaviors as well as skills sets, and pointing out the various dates and times that training and coaching had taken place. Marg was visibly upset, but she continued to listen as Sally spoke. Sally went on to say that she liked Marg, and there were times when Marg did a good job, but it was inconsistent and too much time passing between good performance and poor performance. Then Sally asked Marg if there was something she could help her with; for instance, Sally asked whether Marg is facing personal problems that may be affecting her performance, and then she asked if she was perhaps having difficulties with other people in the office.

After a short pause, Marg started making accusations about others' poor performance and why she was being picked on; she then told Sally that she had not been trained as well as others and that she was not sure she liked working for DS. Sally acknowledged these statements and told her that given the challenges that she would like Marg to take the rest of this Friday off and think about her future with DS over the weekend. Sally went on to say that if Marg wanted to become a member of the team that she would like her to do so but her performance had to improve. For instance, pointing fingers at others would have to stop; she would have to take responsibility for her actions and behaviors, and want to work at DS and with Sally. Sally then assured her that she would make another attempt at training and coaching Marg, but if things were not better after 45 days, Marg would be terminated. Sally then sent Marg home for the rest of the day.

I spoke with Sally about what I called my 3-Day Rule:

Option 1: Marg was going to be angry for three days. On the fourth day, Marg would do a "180-degree turnaround and improve." She might still be quiet due to the "sting," but Sally was to sit with her and do the necessary "clean-up work" of reestablishing a relationship and acknowledging the obvious signs Marg was exhibiting.

Option 2: Marg was going to be angry and quit within the 3-day time frame, very often the next day. By the way, when an employee leaves, it is better than termination because the employer significantly reduces the litigation issue and usually doesn't have to pay unemployment benefits.

Option 3: Marg was going to be angry for three days but return to work and pretend to improve, but go "underground" and consciously or subconsciously sabotage herself and the organization and create problems. In this case, we would monitor her behaviors and know about these adverse actions, make notations in her file, and swiftly terminate.

Another method that works very well and can often increase the likelihood of success and help the employee through this difficult time is to explain the 3-day rule to her before she leaves the room. Go through each example. Then explain that if she chooses option 3, then Sally would find out very quickly and terminate her. It must be expressed at this point that Sally will do everything within her power to train and coach Marg and help her overcome these challenges. Psychologically this process puts the employee in a double bind situation once she realizes she is going through these steps, and it tends to make the person either angrier or short-circuits the process and encourages growth. When the employee realizes that the manager is three steps ahead and knows what the employee is going to do before the employee, this tends to reduce or extinguish the maladaptive behavior. In other words, no matter what decision the employee makes, it has already been thought out and predetermined by her employer.

Termination is devastating for a department or organization due to the ripple effect. In essence, it can uproot concerns about job security within the natural employee population. Termination reverberates throughout an organization, and if some employees do not know the stories behind why a certain employee was dismissed, then all they understand is what they are told by the very efficient grapevine. Therefore, it is imperative to create an organization of trust and communication. Even though management cannot discuss the termination, if employees have built trust with management and if communication channels are secure with regular dialogue, then the little bit of negative gossip should not hurt anything and most employees will say "what took you so long." Employees are very observant, and even though they may like someone, it does not mean they do not know that the person is a slacker or causes ripples in other ways. Very often most employees have tried to coach their friends and tell them "you better be careful how far you push

Susan; you have already been written up two times in the last six weeks." Therefore, all three steps of training, coaching, and counseling must be done with the full intent of helping the employee and the relationship improve.

In this instance, Marg was angry for three days and on day four when she returned, she spun 180° and worked to become a model employee. Three years later she was still employed by Sally and DS Inc. This tactic saved Marg's job, even though it was initially tough for her.

- Sally saved an employee that was coachable and counselable.
- Sally learned to face her fears of conflict and address issues with more confidence and sooner.
- Each time Sally met conflicts, faced her fears, and addressed those issues quicker, she became a better manager. Also, Sally was able to retain more employees and reduce training costs.

As I have alluded to many times leading up to this chapter, when a manager uses force or some fear-based change method, it is imperative to do what's called "clean-up work." When employees have come face to face with hard information, such that it smacks them in the face, they end up "losing face," and then the manager must recalibrate the relationship and do the necessary "clean-up work." Briefly, I want to once again mention that any pain or punishment should be used sparingly because it is very destructive for the trust factor that is the backbone of an effective manager and employee team.

After the third day, the employee should be in a better spot and able to move in one of the three ways. Therefore, it is the job of the manager to address this trust issue between day five and seven after the initial punishment and including the three days of the 3-day rule. The person must have time to acclimate, but not so long as to allow them to feel permanently ridiculed, which will erode trust. This is how you do it.

Sit with the employee and explain that the conversation was tough for you as well as them. The managers must be sincere and communicate their desire to help the employees succeed. Encourage them to express their feelings or frustrations. This will lead to new issues that are problematic, which must be addressed and worked through such as "why didn't you tell me this sooner or you didn't train me properly or I thought I was doing it the way you wanted." These are real concerns and often true since most managers do not address training and coaching issues soon enough, and poor habits are developed and become the norm. When resolved, the list is usually long, since the employee repeated the same process three or more times it became a habit. For him or her to follow so, any criticism comes across as extreme and can often be taken very personal, and finger-pointing back and forth can take place, so be aware of these very real concerns. Therefore, the manager must have the awareness and strong ego strength to accept the issue and express that, "yes, I am learning how to become better at managing just as you are becoming better at your job," which leads to a dialogue about how we communicate sooner and more efficiently.

The symptom was the poor performance, but the real underlying problem was that the manager did not address the issues soon enough, often due to fear of conflict. However, in trying to reduce conflict, they made the conflict more debilitating and cumbersome to deal with. The solution to this is proper training, coaching, counseling, and addressing these issues sooner, which I wrote about earlier in this chapter.

Termination

If a manager cannot improve performance and behavior after training, coaching, and counseling, then it is best for both parties to terminate the business relationship. Therefore, as the manager moves through the first three stages of development, he/she documents all discussions; make a note when an employee has missed the marks and what you and she have planned for rectifying the situation. Be sure to speak with your HR professional about what documents you and the employee need to sign during this entire procedure to make this process fair and legal for both parties. Below are some additional learning components:

1. Frequent interaction and stronger relationships improve trust, which leads to better solutions in less time because people feel free to discuss problems, not just successes, with the manager (Graves 2015).
2. "Employees quit their bosses, not their companies. Good communication translates into less turnover and improved quality and production because long-term employees typically are more efficient and therefore contribute to greater profit" (Graves 2015).
3. When an employee must be terminated, the manager needs to take a minimum of 25% of the blame due to these five points:
   a. The manager hired the wrong person in the first place. Usually, this is caused by not doing your due diligence or in hiring only for skill

set and not accounting for behavior requirements for the position, e.g., the position requires 50 hours a week due to traveling between office branches, and the newly hired employee has a family he is devoted to and is used to a 9–5 schedule.

b. The manager hired the right person but didn't train, coach, and counsel the employee thoroughly enough or soon enough. Also, when problems arose, the manager kept quiet and didn't make as big a deal as should have been made over the issue.

c. The manager inherited a poor performer and didn't develop trust and establish a communication channel that could withstand the pressures of the changeover. Moreover, the manager may not have taken the time with his/her staff to do the necessary development that is required with inherited staff. He/she moved too quickly, and the employees did not have a chance to truly develop trust. One must maintain one-half step to one step ahead of an employee. If the manager goes faster, a chasm is created, and the employee falls behind, and they both lose.

d. A manager inherited a good employee but, due to poor management skills, turned him/her sour on the manager, the department, and perhaps even the organization.

e. The manager was afraid to address issues quickly and honestly because conflict scares him/her, and he/she has not gone through the steps to learn how to deal with conflict effectively.

Benefits of Conflict

Yes, there are many advantages to conflict. It is necessary to struggle through normal stages of business growth, but most people do not know how and stay mired in the muck. The value is in understanding conflict and learning how to harness the elusive powers of this (sometimes) volatile force. As with most challenges, the key is in catching it quickly so you learn to control it before it goes underground (via the grapevine) and causes more problems. Alternatively, worse, it becomes part of your company culture. Many owners, leaders, managers, and employees cannot seem to function without drama or conflict, and, over time, conflict becomes a way of life— unless something significant is done to turn it around. To understand the benefits of conflict, you first need to understand the three main types of conflict.

Types of Conflict

"I've observed three major types of workplace conflict:

Task conflict. Task conflict arises between members of work teams and affects the goals they are striving to achieve. Differences in vision, intentions, and quality expectations often lead to task conflict. Departments, colleagues, and employee relationships may initially appear to survive task conflict, but an important project may not. It is essential to channel task conflict so that these differences become complementary and improve the way the team thinks about accomplishing current and future tasks.

Process conflict. This form of the conflict centers around the steps or methods used by work groups to reach a goal. One person might like to plan twelve steps ahead, while another might like to dive in head first. Process differences can lead to communication breakdown and ultimately result in conflict. Like task conflict, process conflict can be useful if managed correctly. Healthy differences in the process often result in an improved way of achieving challenging goals. In the example, given I have found it best to break them into two teams and have them work from each end in toward the center and compare notes.

Relationship conflict. Often misunderstood, relationship conflict undermines and tears at the fabric of an organization, department, or team's ability to achieve its goals. Relationship conflict penetrates all aspects of an organization. When people in a work environment fail to communicate often and more efficiently, teams, departments, or entire organizations will suffer. Relationship conflict will quickly consume all the attention and energy of an organization, leaving little time to accomplish profitable goals. Catch it quickly and sit the parties down to discuss the friction between them. More than 90 percent of the time, I have found that the culprits in relationship conflict are misperception, misunderstanding, or jumping to conclusions. Have a third-party facilitator break the topics into bite-sized pieces until the misperception can be identified. Then take steps to repair the relationship by having each person name three skills they admire in the other person. Once the core misunderstanding is clarified and removed, this becomes easier than you might initially think" (Graves 2016b).

Resolution

"What can you do to bring the conflict to a reasonable resolution? How might a decision be beneficial to everyone involved? The ultimate goal of resolving conflict is to increase everyone's understanding of what happened, why it happened, and what can be learned from it, so it does not happen again. Conflict is not bad. In fact, it is a vital part of a successful company. Knowing when to encourage conflict in a manageable and productive way, knowing how to spot it early and slow it down if necessary, and knowing the natural stages of conflict's life cycle can all lead to highly productive outcomes. Knowledge about conflict and the skills needed to manage it successfully are necessary to get the best out of yourself and your team" (Graves 2016b).

Significant reduction in liability due to wrongful termination: Organizations that have used my model keep employees longer. However, when an employee is in the "red zone," he/she knows it ahead of time and often resigns. If the issue does go to litigation, the records that have been kept related to specific improvement plans and all the steps taken will make it improbable that any attorney would take the former employee's case. If someone does assume the case, the substantial documentation will provide everything needed for a clear win for the employer's attorney.

Your conscience will be clear knowing you did everything in your power to help your employee be successful.

Our culture has recently moved into a new era where people value camaraderie over individualism. Marketing or promoting "teamwork" without substance to back it up only insults and antagonizes employees. Embracing camaraderie through intelligent leveraging of teamwork and employee/ manager development will make your career more enjoyable and much more successful, and will get you noticed as the magic leader whom employees respect and perform well under.

Summary

When Darwin first made famous the term "survival of the fittest" I do not believe he was talking about the strongest species or the fastest but rather those species most able to adapt quickly to changing surroundings.

Beliefs form through a combination of experience, environment, and the meaning we make out of both. Beliefs can be changed through experiences and authority figures that challenge an existing mindset in a supportive setting. In essence, one's beliefs about one's abilities to expand are flexible by shifting their thoughts or mindsets.

Mindset can be defined as a view employees have of their successes, mistakes, fears, and triumphs and plays a pivotal role in an individual's capacity to learn and change. Dweck's work identifies two distinctly different mindsets that have the greatest implications for successful learning and change over the lifespan: the "Fixed Mindset" and the "Growth Mindset."

A growth mindset is when you believe that through your own efforts you can cultivate your personal qualities. A fixed mindset is when one believes human qualities are carved in stone.

It turns out that managers with a fixed mindset tend to demoralize everyone, including themselves. On the other hand, those with a growth mindset were more data-driven, less anchored by past impressions, and therefore more capable of providing an accurate and unbiased appraisal of employee performance.

Use a growth mindset while developing employees using Allan Weiss' four steps of developing employees. These are:

1. We train employees.
2. We coach employees. Moreover, hopefully, this is where it stops!
3. When employees have personal problems laced with emotional issues, we do our best to help counsel them back to health. When done effectively, they move back into the training and coaching model of development.
4. If managers have done their best at training, coaching, and counseling the employee, then it is both a relief and healthier for the employee and the organization to part company. Therefore, the last stage is termination.

The brutally honest truth is this: It is virtually impossible to have happy external customers when you have unhappy internal customers, i.e., employees! Every point of contact made by an unhappy employee will negatively impact the external customer relationship.

I've observed three major types of workplace conflict (Graves 2016b):

Task conflict. Task conflict arises between members of work teams and affects the goals they are striving to achieve. Differences in vision, intentions, and quality expectations often lead to task conflict.

Process conflict. This form of conflict centers around the steps or methods used by work groups to reach a goal.

Relationship conflict. Often misunderstood, relationship conflict undermines and tears at the fabric of an organization, department, or team's ability to achieve its goals. Catch it quickly and sit the parties down to discuss the friction between them.

Resolution

What can you do to bring the conflict to a reasonable resolution? How might a decision be beneficial to everyone involved? The ultimate goal of resolving conflict is to increase everyone's understanding of what happened, why it happened, and what can be learned from it, so it does not happen again. Conflict is not bad. In fact, it is a vital part of a successful company. Knowing when to encourage conflict in a manageable and productive way, knowing how to spot it early and slow it down if necessary, and knowing the natural stages of conflict's life cycle can all lead to highly productive outcomes (Graves 2016b).

Chapter 6

Gain Competitive Advantage through Transformative Behaviors

Most choices we make daily may be considered well-thought-out decisions. But they are not. They are habits. Although each specific habit may not mean much on its own, over time, the habits like the employee we choose to dislike or pick on, the people we choose to have coffee with in the morning, and the product we order because we think it's a good seller even though the sales data prove us wrong; basically, our daily work routines have enormous impact on the functioning of our team, department, and organization.

The brain must compute millions of emotional, physical, and intellectual computations every day. To streamline this process, the brain uses a technique called "chunking." Chunking is where the brain converts a series of behaviors or actions into automatic routines. A very simple example of chunking is used by the telephone company by breaking the numbers into three sections: the area code, the prefix, and the actual number. This chunking sequence makes numbers much easier for the average learner to commit to memory.

Human memory styles. People's brains memorize different kinds of life events and data at various levels of functioning. For example, some remember facts and numbers better than experiences and tasks and vice versa. See Figure 6.1 and find your memorization preference.

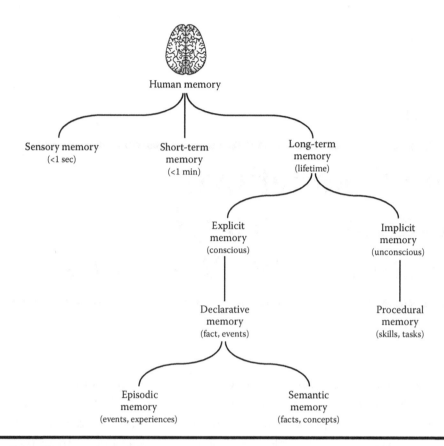

Figure 6.1   Human memory.

Even when the brain is allowed to wander aimlessly, it will automatically start turning most any routine into a habit, because habits allow our minds to concentrate on fewer items. For instance, if you have an "open-door policy" and you allow an employee to come in, sit down, and start telling you about their frustrations or problems three or more times, you have inadvertently taught them to maintain that behavior because you chose not to speak up and establish boundaries. You may have thought you were a good listener, but if you have higher priorities to deal with than hearing about departments not sharing the forklift, then you must make better choices and be quicker at it. Don't languish.

Over time, all animals develop a habit loop, and humans are no different. The psychological discovery by Ivan Pavlov from the famous Pavlov dog experiments was the first of its kind to notice that when the experimenter's assistant entered the room (stimulus), the dogs would salivate (response). In essence, they associated the assistant with food, and before receiving food, the dog would salivate over the impending food (Figure 6.2).

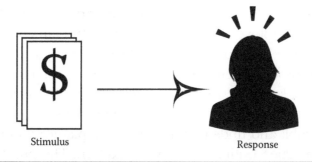

Figure 6.2   Stimulus response.

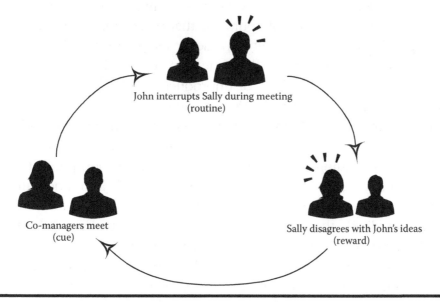

Figure 6.3   Habit loop.

The habit loop consists of three parts (refer to Figure 6.3). First, there is the cue, a trigger that tells your brain to go into automatic mode and which habit to use. Next, there is the routine, which consists of either the mental, emotional, or physical. And finally, there is the reward, which helps one's brain determine if this particular loop is worth remembering to follow in the future (Duhigg 2012).

Over extended periods of time, this habit loop consisting of the cue, routine, and reward becomes more instinctive and slowly becomes a habit. Eventually, something as simple as where you tend to park at work becomes a habit. You may refer to it as logical or convenient, but it's becoming ingrained into your subconscious and placed onto the hard drive of your long-term memory.

The reason why the discovery of the habit loop is so vital to developing yourself and your employees is that it presents a fundamental law: When a habit solidifies, the brain disengages and stops fully participating in the decision-making process. Remember, the body is extremely efficient in the energy it expends, so when a habit develops, the brain diverts resources to other parts of the body for other tasks. The problem is, unless one purposely fights a habit and finds new routines, the pattern will go back to its previous baseline cue, routine, and reward pattern. The problem is habits never leave us.

Once firmly established, habits never disappear. They are encoded into our long-term memory, so when we need to summon them, they immediately appear. The problem, of course, is that one's brain can't decipher between good habits or ones that don't serve us. As a result, if one has a bad habit, it's waiting just under the surface to rise for the cue like a trout to a fly. How might a negative, bad, or unproductive habit hurt our career?

For example, if John and Sally are co-managers, and they meet (cue) with the other managers, John typically bullies the conversation and interrupts or speaks over Sally (the routine). This, in turn, aggravates Sally, and she retaliates by arguing or shooting down every idea John presents even if she begrudgingly agrees with it (reward). At best, both John and Sally are viewed by the other managers as troublemakers and difficult to work with. At worst, they divide the team in an "us versus them" (Graves 2016b) quiet battle where people, departments, and even divisions can work against each other. This makes it that much easier for the competition, which is smart enough to remove these habits to gain a competitive advantage.

Beliefs, in short, are just rules for action, and the whole function of thinking is but one step in the production of habits of action.

Habit Change: Replacing Old Habits with New

The key to managing a successful team is to change their automatic habits, but how does one do this? By making their processes automatic, in essence, to take the thinking out of the smaller decisions (this is the reason why *core values* are so important). They create rules whereby the executive, manager, and employee can make favorable decisions by using the matrix of the core values, thereby making the rare and complex habitually uncomplicated. If a manager can instill the right process and decision-making habits, as a by-product, his or her team will be more successful.

Successful organizations and departments don't do the extraordinary thing; they do ordinary things, but they do them the same way each time without thinking. They follow and repeat the habits they have learned.

Remember, one can never fully extinguish an unproductive habit. Rather, to change a habit, one must keep the old cue and deliver the old reward but insert a new routine. This is a simple truism: if one uses the same cue, and provides the same reward, one can shift the routine and change the habit (Duhigg 2012).

Beliefs are critical. One must think change is possible before the behavior will follow. This is the basis for why a shared vision, mission, and core values and objectives are essential.

Even if you provide new and better habits, that in and of itself will not change the routine. Eventually a bad day or lost deal will make a negative impact on the person or team, and they will likely go back to baseline or old habits. The secret sauce is believing they can change their routines and habits. If they did it once, they could do it again. One key ingredient is using the power of the group.

There is something powerful about teams and their shared experiences. By themselves, people may be skeptical and lose momentum, but when aligned with others who are focused on the same objectives and perhaps struggling with the same problem, it can make it easier due to the shared experiences of the team. This is the glue that makes teams stronger: the community struggle.

Once people struggle together and win or achieve a milestone, then this works as a solidifying moment. When this team more often pushes themselves out of their comfort zone and succeeds, then they start to believe in themselves and one another on a much deeper level. This is when the company culture starts to shift. "Cultures revolve around success" (Schein 2010), and when they view more often themselves as successful, and this has been reinforced, then it becomes rewarding. When people are part of a team where change seems possible, the potential for that change to occur becomes more real.

Have you ever met people that you and others considered "lucky"? It seems that no matter what happens to them, it somehow always turns out well. Conversely, have you heard people say "life is lousy, and then you die" or "bad things always happen to me"? the very thing that limits people's abilities in life is their deeply held beliefs. In other words, if people see themselves as lucky and capable, they are right, and if they see themselves as unlucky and deficient, they are also right.

People see what they intend to see, hear what they intend to hear, and gravitate toward the mental image they have of themselves. Once these thoughts are imprinted, then parallel action, statements, and behaviors follow—whether they are helpful or harmful. Deeply held beliefs can also be thought of as a "self-fulfilling prophecy" and, when positively leveraged using mental imagery, can become a powerful tool.

Athletes have been using mental imagery to improve their performance for years. You have probably seen athletes with their eyes closed imagining driving a racecar, skiing, or hitting a golf ball. The good news is that everyone from secretaries to CEOs can use this same technique to achieve similar outstanding results in their profession. This method involves mental rehearsal before the actual event, so the actions, statements, and behaviors can follow suit. The more precise and often one practices mental imaging, the higher the probability one has of achieving it. Steps to practice mental imagery are as follows:

1. *Relax*: Close your eyes and relax, then visualize yourself achieving the goal, i.e., hitting a golf ball squarely, running a timely and goal-oriented meeting, executing improved performance evaluations, making decisions and confidently sticking with them, or maintaining a positive behavior.

2. *End result*: Picture the "result," i.e., in what ways will people benefit from your meetings, how will the department and employees benefit from goal-oriented performance reviews, how might you experience life once your mood is more consistent?

3. *Experience it*: Begin to picture and feel what it "will" be like to experience your objective.
   a. How do you look to others? Confident, in control of the situation, skilled.
   b. How will you feel when you are fully experiencing your objective? A personal sense of accomplishment, relaxed, proud yet humble, happy, and excited.
   c. How is your body and mind responding? Alert, responsive, insightful, strong, capable, in touch with others.

4. *Others' response*: Visualize how others will respond to your behavior, i.e., thankful for a productive meeting, grateful to you for creating a safe environment for them to share ideas and contribute to the group, or shaking your hand for creating the department they always hoped was possible.

5. *Your response*: Visualize your response based upon their response to you, i.e., appreciated, valued, thankful, pleased, accomplished, knowing you can do this more often.
6. *Execute*: Open your eyes and store these feelings and thoughts into your long-term memory. Then:
   a. Make a commitment to yourself to practice this visual imaging a set number of times per day or week.
   b. Make it a part of your life and utilize it in different areas of your life.

Everything an athlete does is measured so they can become the best possible. Mental imagery and programming is a vital part of their practice regime. Professional athletes often become successful business people after their sporting career is over, and much of it is attributable to having a clear mental image of their next objective. Our mind is a powerful muscle and, when leveraged in a methodical and consistent basis, can help us achieve our best.

"Keystone habits are habits that matter most" (Duhigg 2012, p. 101). When these start to shift, they inadvertently create other patterns. You may recall from Chapter 3, for example, when problems arose that Timid Tami had trouble speaking directly to her subordinates. She and I worked on being direct and training her new employee every week between Monday and Friday. Eventually, after four weeks, Timid Tami had learned to bring up difficult topics with her subordinates in the moment as issues arose. Tami's skill at addressing issues in the moment became a "keystone habit."

1. You can't order people to change, but when you involve them in the decision making, it becomes significantly easier.
2. By attacking one habit and then watching the changes ripple through the department.
3. Identify one key process that needs changing.
4. Disrupt that process or key habit and focus on changing it.
5. Remember that changing the routine works as a lever. But the ramifications act as a pebble thrown into a glassy-surfaced pond, where the water ripples outward to the edge where water meets land. And when that water has enough power and force behind it, then it can act like a tsunami and make significant changes within an industry (think of Apple and how its technology changed not one but multiple industries).

MED Review example is a noteworthy keystone habit that when altered can manifest significant changes within an organization. Moreover, the reason why the Manager and Employee review is such a powerful tool is that it permeates every aspect of an organization such as

- Frequency of communication between the manager and the employee
- Specificity of topic and breaks these issues into smaller bite-sized pieces
- Creates an environment of trust and dialogue with its equilibrium-focused format
- Outlines specific follow-up procedures and tasks
- Schedules predetermined times for follow-up
- And creates mutual participant habits that can be easily repeated

Example

Here is an example of how one can significantly change an organization in a matter of weeks or a few short months. CR is in the construction business and over the last 50 years had grown from one office to five. Most of that growth had come in the last eight years when the second-generation CEO decided to open branch offices in the same region. Due to this rapid growth, many bad habits had been allowed to manifest such as branch managers not holding people accountable, each branch had its set of rules and processes, and no formal training program. Business was excellent so new employees were thrown into positions to either sink or swim, and many had perished along the way. Dave, the CEO, decided a change was needed and contracted with me to help them. After the initial intake sessions, it was agreed that the quickest way to help this organization achieve their goals and make the changes necessary was to implement the MED Review.

Our plan was to spend an entire day with each branch manager every month with weekly 30- to 60-minute phone conversations during the off weeks. In the first round, Dave and I met with each branch manager and had an honest discussion around top priorities. Between the branch manager, Dave, and myself, we helped reprioritize the manager's duties. One example is rather than doing so much of his or her project manager's work for them (being just another pair of PM hands), the three of us trained, coached, and counseled the project manager. We decided that the top areas that would yield the most ROI would be

1. Writing project and insurance estimates
2. Daily discussions about the projects and keeping everyone in the communication loop
3. How to train, coach, and counsel those employees below them

We trained them to do better project and insurance estimates; we trained them how to meet every morning to outline the plans with their superintendents and then how to train those below them. Our objective was to keep the steps to each process simple. Going back to the model, all we had to do was consistently help them change their daily routine to achieve significant growth.

At first, branch managers and project managers said they didn't have time to train, coach, and counsel. As they put it, "we're swamped now, and you want me to take time out of my day to teach, coach, and counsel people; they should just get it." However, Dave and I held to our plan of developing the management team from top to bottom. The first two to three months was difficult, and we had to drop some of the lower-priority projects, which was a learning component. CR had always taken every insurance job that came through the door, and many were not profitable and simply added to the frustration and anxiety.

Second, we added to the bonus structure to include all the project managers as a unit. All their gross margins had to improve by a certain percentage before anyone got the extra quarterly bonus. We wanted the most experienced estimators to help us teach and coach the less experienced estimators. There was initial grumbling, but the margins grew so well that after the second quarter, all PMs were making more money and connecting more frequently with all the other PMs at different branches. This, in turn, created a more inclusive organizational culture, even though some of the branches were more than 200 miles apart. Interestingly enough, the PMs started coaching one another on other challenges as in how to deal more effectively with the insurance companies. This automatically helped with our second objective, which was to improve communication within and between branches, and where some people were better at estimating projects, others were better with people issues and managing others, so a significant level of cross-development took place.

By changing one routine, we received the benefit of improving all three of our objectives. All that Dave, the branch managers, and I had to do were help facilitate conversations on the front end and debrief output on the back end. Last we helped the group learn about their learning and encouraged them to engage more frequently in this process.

Habit Modification Plan

"One paper published by Duke University researcher found that over 40% of the actions people performed each day were not actual conscious decisions but rather unconscious habits" (Duhigg 2012, p. xvi). Once aware of undesirable habits in oneself or others, specific techniques can be used to alter this automatic sequence. One cannot change or extinguish behaviors and habits automatically. Like asking someone to think of "nothing," it's impossible or nearly so. However, as smart moms have known for years, unruly conduct can be redirected to more acceptable activities when done consistently and positively reinforced. In other words, undesirable behaviors and habits can be reprogramed if the sequence outlined next is followed religiously.

These techniques have been successfully applied in many diverse situations and industries. "For instance, NFL Coach Tony Dungy used this method to turn the Tampa Bay Buccaneers into one of the league's most winning teams. Dungy would become the only coach in NFL history to reach the playoffs ten consecutive years and the first African-American coach to win the Super Bowl. From 1986 to 1996 Paul O'Neil took Alcoa chemical from a company with union friction, a terrible safety record and substandard profits to an organization that got high marks from leadership, employees and unions while improving the stock price over 200%" (Duhigg 2012, pp. 60–153). When Howard Schultz took back control of Starbucks, he hired psychologists to teach Starbucks trainers to use this method to train all of its employees how to effectively satisfy customers, especially the frustrated. Starbucks may have good coffee, but what sets them apart from the thousands of competitors is their outstanding customer service. These methods work equally for improving exercise routines as they do on shop floors and in boardrooms. The secret is consistency. If you apply them consistently, you and your organization will grow.

I will use an example that all business people are familiar with: the loud bully who interrupts and inadvertently turns business meetings into a nightmare. Habit Reversal Training was researched and developed in part by Nathan Azrin, PhD.

1. Make a list of the behaviors or habits the client or team would like to modify or improve.
   a. Example: Tim takes over the meeting with his loud and domineering voice and often interrupts others.
2. Create a T-graph and list the precise behaviors observed or statements heard on the left side of the page. On the right side, list potential competing behaviors used to interrupt the routine.
   a. Example: Left side of the graph—Tim takes over the meeting with his loud and domineering voice and often interrupts others.

    b. Example: Right side of the graph—The official leader and others within the group are encouraged to "verbally acknowledge the unproductive behavior and statements." "Tim, are you aware that when you speak loud and interrupt, the meetings take longer and the team doesn't gain the best solutions, which cost all of us time and money?"

3. The group counts the number of times per meeting, day, week, or month the harmful behavior is occurring (record on white board, index cards, or in a notebook that can be referred to).

4. Awareness training; response description procedure.
    a. The client is to describe in detail the detrimental habit or behavior.
    b. The facilitator is to observe and *punctuate* the sequence by making the participants aware of the harmful habit. In a meeting, participants are encouraged to respectfully catch each other's detrimental habit.
    c. An early warning procedure where the client would detect the earliest signs of the habit/behavior, i.e., negative internal dialogue, tension in shoulders, clenching jaw, raising voice levels, angry tone, finger-pointing, etc.
    d. Situation awareness training in which the client/team lists all the places, people, and circumstances in which the detrimental habit occurred in the past.

5. Competing response training.
    a. Have the person or meeting participants describe what they could do to avert the negative interactions or responses. This must come from the person and not the facilitator since each person understands their internal dialogue and metaphors better than anyone else. In the case of the "meeting bully," how could the team assist this individual in applying new behaviors that would replace or override the detrimental habit? Often, by simply broaching this topic in a straightforward manner, the "meeting bully" will not be aware of their behaviors or feign ignorance. In any case, the subject is broached, and they will often ask for help. The facilitator can then ask, "when you take over or interrupt, what would you like the group to do to help you?" They often say "tell me right then." The facilitator says, "I imagine with history, people may be reluctant. I know I might be if I were in their shoes." So, in that event, what if you try to overpower them and increase your assertiveness? What do you suggest? Again, the bully often says, "bring it to my attention; then we can practice a few times."

    b. Each client is taught competing responses. For instance, with shoulder tension, one would overly tense the shoulder muscles and hold for 60 seconds then release. Repeat exercise. Every time, the tension arises, do immediate physical activity. Become acutely aware of the habit and quickly replace every time.

    c. For cognitive people, create a flow chart, such as if "A" happens, then choose between precreated options "B" or "C" to replace the harmful habit immediately (Figure 6.4).

6. Habit control motivation.

    a. Replacing habits is hard work and requires constant attention. The first step in this process measures motivation to change. I suggest the 0–10 scale, where 0 equals no motivation and 10 equals maximum motivation.

    b. For instance, if you rated your motivation at "5," ask yourself why it is "5" rather than a "3" or "4." This technique will provide insight into how you are currently successful (5) in your motivation.

    c. Apply inconvenience habit report. How has this detrimental practice been hurting you and your team? Stunted job advancement, job loss, task deficiency, team/department turmoil. List them.

    d. Reinforce small successes to improve frequency.

    e. Frequently debrief what works and apply solution techniques.

7. Long-term habit formation.

    a. A visual measurement device such as wall/whiteboard, meeting scheduler, calendar and measure improved frequency by day, week, and month.

Over time and with consistent effort, evolution takes place and transformation is achieved.

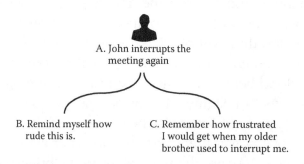

Figure 6.4   Habit training. Cognitive people.

Successful Target Behaviors to Create Stellar Habits

Below is a list of behaviors successful managers need to be practicing at various levels within an organization. Compare your behaviors and those of your direct reports to the list, then train and coach yourself and others toward the target behaviors.

Feedback and Learning

Continuously learns from experiences. Seeks out feedback and development opportunities. Builds awareness of strengths and development needs. Shares knowledge and experiences with others.

Team member:

- Proactively evaluates own skills and knowledge
- Identifies own strengths and areas for development
- Asks for and accepts feedback about own performance in the job
- Willingly takes on and learns new skills
- Shares knowledge and experience
- Builds upon and learns from experiences
- Identifies, documents, and shares knowledge that might be useful to others
- Seeks out developmental opportunities (new projects, training, work with experienced and knowledgeable professional)
- Sets goals for own development

Manager/senior manager:

- Identifies lessons learned from challenging incidents
- Puts procedures in place to avoid common problems from occurring again
- Develops, updates, and follows own personal development plan
- Helps others to learn from the day-to-day experience, not just formal training
- Encourages others to share experiences and learn from each other
- Actively gathers knowledge, lessons from experience, and learning from external sources
- Seeks feedback from all levels and from customers/clients and acts on that feedback

Director:

- Anticipates development areas to meet new challenges
- Identifies where the most value can be delivered in the director role

Executive leadership:

- Anticipates new development areas to meet future challenges
- Identifies where the most value can be delivered in own role
- Reinvents and adapts own role to fit the changing needs of the organization

Developing People

Gives clear directions, positive and constructive feedback. Coaches less experienced staff. Actively develops or assists the development of others.

Team member:

- Shares appropriate credit for successes (informs more senior staff of others' successes)
- Acts as a peer adviser to new team members
- Gives timely feedback to others
- Provides clear directions to others
- Coaches and supports others when appropriate

Manager/senior manager:

- Gives others the opportunity to take on new tasks and responsibilities
- Establishes and manages a clear set of standards for others to work within
- Encourages others to get the most out of their development opportunities
- Evaluates performance and takes appropriate action
- Manages the expectations of people regarding career development and progression
- Recognizes and develops potential so that the team has the necessary knowledge, skills, and experience

- Empowers staff with the appropriate responsibilities to be able to work autonomously
- Develops people who have potential and those who have development needs
- Identifies and enables career progression of high-potential people
- Gains the trust and respect of staff at all levels
- Brings clarity to the work of others—focuses on their effort and commitment

Director:

- Anticipates future skill requirements within own discipline and builds these in the team
- Creates formal development opportunities for others, beyond those provided by day-to-day work
- Challenges others to seize development opportunities

Executive leadership:

- Supports high performance by providing adequate resources and structures
- Sets challenging and stretching goals for own department/organization to follow
- Brings people from functional and geographical boundaries together to commit to shared goals

Summary

Most choices we make daily may be considered well-thought-out decisions. But they are not. They are habits. Although each specific habit may not mean much on its own, over time, the habits like the employee we choose to dislike or pick on, the people we choose to have coffee with in the morning, and the product we order because we think it's a good seller even though the sales data prove us wrong; basically our daily work routines have enormous impact on the functioning of our team, department, and organization.

Over time all animals develop a habit loop, and humans are no different. The habit loop consists of three parts. First, there is the cue, a trigger that tells your brain to go into automatic mode and which habit to use. Next, there is the routine, which consists of either the mental, emotional, or physical. And finally, there is the reward, which helps one's brain determine if this particular loop is worth remembering to follow in the future.

The reason why the discovery of the habit loop is so vital to developing yourself and your employees is that it presents a fundamental law: When a habit solidifies, the brain disengages and stops fully participating in the decision-making process.

Remember, one can never fully extinguish an unproductive habit. Rather, to change a habit, one must keep the old cue and deliver the old reward but insert a new routine. This is a simple truism: if one uses the same cue, and provides the same reward, one can shift the routine and change the habit. Keystone habits are habits that matter most. When these start to shift, they inadvertently create stronger reinforcing patterns.

Beliefs are critical. One must think change is possible before the behavior will follow. This is the basis for why a shared vision, mission, and core values and objectives are essential.

There is something powerful about teams and their shared experiences. Once people struggle together and win or achieve a milestone, then this works as a solidifying moment. When this team more often pushes themselves out of their comfort zone and succeeds, then they start to believe in themselves and one another on a much deeper level. This is when the company culture starts to shift. Cultures revolve around success, and when they more often view themselves as successful, and this has been reinforced, then it becomes rewarding.

DEPARTMENT DEVELOPMENT LEADS TO COMPANY SUCCESS

Chapter 7

How to Develop
Evolutionary Teams

Organizational skills and behaviors are the way a collective group of people representing an organization demonstrates who they are through action. The manifestation of these is critical to the success of all organizations and demonstrates a company's willingness to translate thought, theory, and planning into action (Schein 2010).

The evolved manager identifies and pursues business opportunities by teaching and coaching his or her employees about

- The commercial context of their product and services
- How the processes of the organization function to make it more efficient
- Internal and external clients and why we must take care of both equally
- Our competitors, markets, and the external environment
- The organizational strategy, financial targets, and what their department must do to help the organization achieve its long-term objectives and short-term goals

For this to take place, the evolved manager must develop each employee so that he or she works toward and thinks about

- Building an understanding of the client/customer business such as the issues they face, the markets they operate in, and key developments
- The latest trends in our market, including competitor activity
- Possible business opportunities and advises manager of these

A good manager does the following:

■ Links the activities of the department to the firm's business strategy
■ Respectfully questions current practices in relation to own department by thinking about the longer-term impact and wider implications
■ Emphasizes and builds the value of products and/or services offered to the customer
■ Uses research into customer businesses (the issues they face, the state of new markets, key developments) to initiate new service and/or product offerings
■ Finds opportunities to develop future business from existing customer engagements
■ Identifies and acts upon business opportunities
■ Develops productive internal and external relationships that promote business

An evolved manager uses those mentioned above as well as these:

■ Explains organization's business focus, targets, and guidelines, providing clarity about the implications for his or her team and how it impacts each individual
■ Gathers and shares market knowledge and intelligence with his or her team as well as with his or her colleagues
■ Uses understanding of the market to make sure that new product and service offerings are aligned with customer/client needs
■ Acts as a champion for the organization's initiatives
■ Takes a broad view of customer/client needs, looking beyond own area of experience and know-how
■ Develops long-term focused plans to help maximize commercial success and updates them to capitalize on developments
■ Seizes opportunities to extend breadth and depth of products and services
■ Focuses on activities that will deliver the greatest long-term return

Steps to Developing the Team

The process I have been writing about in previous chapters works as well for groups of people or teams as it does for individuals. A system, whether that be an individual, small group, or large organization, has many similarities as you will see as we continue to work our way through this chapter.

A successful team is more than a group of people working with one another. Here is a list describing the thoughts of each member of this elite class of super professionals dedicated to their goals:

1. High commitment
2. High levels of trust
3. Desire to achieve as a group
4. Not only understanding one another's strengths and weaknesses but excited by this knowledge and able to leverage the former while making up for the latter
5. Dedication to self-development

High commitment from each member of the team is vital. A team cannot move to the next stages of growth without commitment. If one member is not committed, it is best to replace them rather than hope their skill set will outweigh their dedication to the group. Skills can be taught, commitment cannot.

As I have mentioned many times in this book, for a group of people to evolve into a team, trust must be the bedrock upon which they build their relationships. Colleagues must get to the point where overfiltering of thoughts is reduced and finally eliminated so that the genius can flow unobstructed out to the members. It is this free-flowing of ideas where genius starts to unfold, and one person's idea sparks others and a roaring fire of thought soon erupts creating its own storm of performance-oriented behaviors.

Once the team has created this dynamic two or three times, it becomes invigorating and self-propelling. Colleagues start trying to repeat the magic every time they come together, and the more often they practice, the more often this magic appears.

As a team evolves, they become acutely aware of one another's strengths and weaknesses, and these traits become less obtrusive. Members make adjustments for each other, and differences become strengths as the team instinctively knows who to rely on given the nature of the problem to be solved. For instance, Kendall is the CEO and excellent at seeing a market niche and rallying the team to go after it. He has vision and unwavering commitment to achieving objectives. However, Kendall can get so caught up in his tunnel vision that he overlooks details such as budgets and realistic time frames. Kevin, on the other hand, is a gifted CFO and excellent at taking Kendall's ideas and budgeting for them, while Brandon's strength is planning and logistics. Of course each of these men has overlapping strengths, but when the chips are down and every move counts, this team relies on the skills of their specialists to make the call in their given field.

The toughest of these five is one's ability to be self-aware and introspective. It is vital to the success of the team for each member to look within himself/herself and self-correct when he/she falters. Likewise, it is imperative for the members to acknowledge a member's mistake and build him/her up despite it. It goes without saying that the member who made a mistake knows about it and will take the necessary steps to correct the deficiency. Being berated by any member only weakens the bond and flow of the team. Case in point: when a wide receiver misses a pass, no one needs to remind him or berate him during the game. It is history; move on to the next play, and don't allow the past to upset the future.

The Morning Huddle

People become complacent after they have done things for a while and expect each work day to be a repeat of the previous day or week. This will lull you into making big mistakes that are quite easily fixed. The morning huddle is a great way to start each day whether you are in an office or down on the shop floor. People need to connect, be reminded of the goals, and be aware of slight changes that may have taken place. For example, due to changing conditions, our number six priority has now moved into the number one position. It may be as simple as discussing the number of packages to be shipped that day or the run of parts being made that must be ready for shipping by tomorrow at 3 p.m.

Morning huddles are designed to be quick, direct, and to the point just like in football. What are the goals for the next four to eight hours in a warehouse or production line, and which branch office need the most help this week or to debrief the previous day's events?

Some teams choose to do a "check-in." A check-in is where each person takes 15 to 60 seconds and shares their need for the day, i.e., if they are not feeling well or one might be up to date on his/her work so he/she can help others should they need it. Evolutionary teams have learned the 5 minutes spent huddling or checking in is paid back 100 times each day as needs and events change because the member population of the team is tight among themselves. They are forced to learn how to communicate frequently, quickly, and efficiently.

Executives may balk at the misperceived time waste and the employees may see it as redundant, but the evolutionary manager knows how to spend time and resources wisely and knows the ROI he/she receives from huddles. In addition, the evolutionary manager attains performance heights others can't duplicate so leaders tend to leave him/her alone. The smart manager prepares for his/her huddle.

The huddle of 15 people may take only 7 minutes, but the preparation the manager must do may take up to three to four times if he/she gathers information from other departments and condenses it into a format his/her employees need and will hear. An example is telling his/her employees that they received an extra 3,000 orders last night, and so they must figure out how to have them ready for the two UPS shipments coming today at 3 p.m. and 7 p.m., so that they make their 24-hour delivery schedule.

Evolutionary Teams

1. Address issues immediately.
2. Communicate frequently and clearly.
3. Confirm message sent was message received.
4. Outline and discuss clear goals.
5. Create clear time frames for those goals to be achieved. For instance, they say 12 noon, not in the middle of the day.
6. Measure progress.
7. Regularly debrief.
8. Positively reinforce what parts went well and discuss adjusting those that didn't hit the mark.
9. Accept responsibility.
10. Solving problems.

Make no mistake about it; this seems easy, but many managers falter here. Once learned, it's very easy to do and will cut your workload in half. When there is an issue with Paul and Jack or with production and marketing, the best advice is to

1. Gather information from each party (or parties).
2. Ask if you can bring the two of them together for a discussion.

3. Bring them together and help them communicate concerns and successes.
4. Create an environment of communication and trust framed with specific goals.
5. Once complete, ask each person what the one thing was that they got out of the discussion.

The Debrief

Without a doubt, the debrief is the most valuable and least practiced technique. It is seen as a waste of time and mainly not given the time because teams are usually behind so they rush to the next crises. But for those who practice it, it is a vein of gold your competitors will likely miss. The debrief is easy to do.

1. After completing a project, gather the team together into a confined place (The closer people are to one another, the more they will connect. Distance in space determines distance in relationship. The closer, the better.) and discuss what went well and how the team can repeat it. Just focus on repeating the successes. When discussing dropped balls, focus on the tasks or events; don't make it personal and blame. Whoever is facilitating should offer his/her observations as well, but remember that a great debrief requires communication and at first people may not be open to this or feel uncomfortable. Believe me, after they practice this technique three or four times, you will not be able to shut them up.
2. Maintain control of the team and ensure it goes into a productive direction. Don't be too stringent on this rule, but don't allow a person to vent for 10 minutes but rather implement a 60- to 90-second "vent" rule. Encourage a discussion about what people observed about themselves and others, what they thought, how it made them feel. Basically, take them deeper than normal, and you will gain more information than normal.
3. Ask them when they are going to apply this information in the future. Might there be other or new uses for this information? People and their behaviors follow a path of redundancy, so if they behave one way during one project, it is a high probability they will respond close to that in the next project. Learn from this. By doing this you place them mentally into the next project and plant the seed of successful behaviors because they have practiced it once in their mind's eye...with you.

Habits of Smart Teams

1. They meet weekly and discuss tasks such as the following:
   a. Financial numbers and how they relate to the previous week.
   b. HR discusses who was hired and what positions are still open and what people are going through the on-boarding process.
   c. Marketing repeats some of the changes their adjustments are achieving.
   d. Each branch manager shares tasks achieved or those not yet gotten to from the previous week.
   e. The COO asks each person what tasks they completed in relation to the previous week's list.
2. Habits of evolved teams go one level deeper and discuss people, problems, and solutions such as the following:
   a. The manager and staff in our northern regional office have become complacent and need to be developed.
   b. First, we need someone to travel there and gather information so we can determine a baseline.
   c. We need to discuss these issues among the executive team and then with the branch manager and his staff so we can brainstorm possible solutions to bridge the gap.
   d. How are we going to split the duties between the executive team and develop that manager and those below him?
   e. When will we start this endeavor?
   f. What will constitute acceptable success?
   g. What will constitute our target success?
   h. What will be done to follow up and ensure development is maintained after we leave?
   i. How often do we need to measure maintenance progress?

Example: CR, INC Level One Meeting Development

When I arrived, their meetings were task-oriented with strained trust and communication levels.

When I gathered my information from each executive and manager, this is what I heard:

■ People who questioned themselves and their place in the organization.
■ They did not trust to speak openly about what they felt and thought about solutions to correct problems.

- They doubted the direction the organization was going.
- They privately questioned the way in which the CEO, COO, and coexecutives were attempting to fix the problems.
- Lastly, they doubted their ability and personal influence to move the team from where it was to where it needed to be.

These executives knew change was necessary; they had tried many books, workshops, and even a few consultants, but nothing they or others had tried seemed to correct their pain.

Their behaviors I observed that told me this was, in fact, true were the following:

- Arguing among executives and managers
- Finger-pointing at one another
- Competition, defensiveness, and power struggles
- Lack of working together and finding joint solutions
- People who worked hard but never made the progress they thought they should given the amount of effort expended
- Frustration with and anger toward the CEO for not fixing the company
- Loss of interest in their jobs and the company success

The first thing I did was move the CR executive team meetings from task-oriented to development-oriented. The foundation was there; we simply needed to get the best out of the people we had. So, we implemented the outline above by first focusing on

- Taking a step back and working on developing relationships between the executives and managers.
- I had each person talk about their life, what kind of person they were, and how they liked to communicate with others.
- We discussed how to listen while other people were talking rather than thinking of one's response while others were talking.
- We discussed how to give and receive feedback and how past interactions had caused friction and what each person thought at the time versus now after they had shared about themselves.
- We discussed the productive and unproductive ways to approach conflict.

Next, we discussed the different leadership styles required to lead and manage people. At their current stage of development, they required the following:

- Guidance and for their superior to clarify his or her viewpoint if points made were not fully understood.
- We discussed that orders should not be given but explained in a joint fashion. However, after the discussion, the superior still has the authority to make the final decision and the subordinate needs to accept that and fully support it.
- We discussed how relationships are just as important as tasks.

After 60 days of development, the team was starting to make progress and showing signs of an evolved team. When I coached, and listened to the members, I heard statements such as

- I feel I am finally becoming a part of a team.
- We accomplished more now than we did previously, and I understand how I fit into the team and my role.
- As each week goes by, I feel a little more comfortable in expressing my ideas without worrying about them getting shot down.
- I feel there is a deeper sense of trust between my teammates and me; we are becoming a team rather than a group of people working together.
- When there are problems, we now know how to provide constructive criticism to one another.
- I feel the team is finally hitting on all cylinders and that we are not only going to make but achieve our big daring audacious goals.

What I observed during this transition period were

- Members were taking risks and practicing open and honest communication.
- Members would begin an argument and quickly stop themselves, or another person would come to their aid and walk them through the conflict resolution steps.

- Before decisions were made, complex problems were discussed and dissected. Members encouraged each other to speak up and share ideas.
- Even though individuals would make mistakes, the team were making significant progress every week. A healthy balance of power had been developed.
- Members had a well-defined plan, and this clarity gave them purpose and a unified sense of team.
- They achieved the goals they set out to achieve.

We made these major breakthroughs by

- Supporting one another and making this a priority.
- Each member was encouraged to participate, even the quieter members who after they got acclimated became some of the stronger members of the team in relation to great ideas.
- Members continued to hold one another accountable and listen for understanding first and then think of one's response. They practiced listening and made it a top priority knowing if one does not listen correctly, problems arise immediately.

Steps an Evolved Manager Takes to Problem Solving

An evolved manager analyzes problems, identifies core issues, investigates, evaluates and integrates information, and generates appropriate solutions to solve problems or issues.

A good manager solves problems by

- Asking relevant questions to get clarity on key issues
- Evaluates a situation or data based upon the facts, not just upon opinions
- Identifies information gaps and seeks additional information if necessary
- Gathers information from a wide variety of sources relevant to each piece of work
- Checks that information is correct, valid, and comprehensive
- Proposes solutions that solve the core problem or issue

An evolved manager solves problems using the former techniques but adds the following:

- Uses a range of techniques to analyze an issue
- Identifies ways to analyze information quickly and efficiently
- Suggests innovative and creative solutions to problems
- Reviews the accuracy of team members' assumptions
- Initiates smarter ways of working by making improvements to processes and looking for efficiency enhancements
- Provides clear rationale and supporting data to justify recommended solutions
- Considers the practicalities and costs involved when proposing a solution to a problem
- Uses creativity and lateral thinking in solving problems (including far-reaching issues spanning the work of many individuals)
- Integrates information from a variety of different sources and considers the broader impact of issues
- Recognizes trends in complex data
- Challenges teams' assumptions, conclusions, and solutions
- Chooses or recommends from a range of options or possibilities
- Assesses the risks and wider impact of range of different options
- Trains and coaches others by making suggestions and offering ideas on how to approach problems
- Uses own experience and knowledge to help others to generate solutions
- Solves unusual or complex customer/client problems

QUALITY DIGEST—THE BUILDING BLOCKS OF ORGANIZATIONAL PSYCHOLOGY, PART 2 (GRAVES 2015)

In my last article, I presented the psychological steps of change and how to overcome the natural human resistance to it. In this installment, I will present an example of how to transfer those concepts into plans, the plans into actions, and the actions into continuous behaviors.

This process might be considered as a look at the psychological underpinnings of plan-do-check-act (PDCA). This is important because leaders and managers are paid to take action and get results, and that requires people to improve and evolve.

Before management starts to improve a person, department, or manufacturing process, it's a good idea to invite those involved to help solve the problem. Two vital things happen here: (1) Involving people suggests trust in their abilities, which inspires them and encourages confidence and creativity; and (2) Psychologically this makes everyone working to solve this problem part of the same team and removes the "us vs. them" dynamic that often plagues these types of "smart boss, stupid employee" misperceptions.

A Manufacturing Case Study

Company ABC makes mining shovel teeth. Recently, hardness consistency had dropped to a point where 40% of product heated, treated, and quenched was either too hard or too soft, which cost the company about $75,000 a month in scrapped product and rework costs.

Management took a 10-step approach to investigating, implementing, and maintaining changes that would alleviate this situation, as follows:

1. Prioritize objectives. It is necessary to choose one quality metric to measure and improve in a limited period of time (say a single month or quarter). In this case, management decided to look at improving the quench tank process over the next 30 days.
2. Determine target result. This requires specificity; management targeted an improvement in hardness consistency of around 400 and a reduction in scrap loss from 40% down to an acceptable 2%–3%.
3. Asking, "How will improvement in this area help the customer?" Longer wear extends tooth life and provides a better return on the company's investment. Brittle teeth break and go through the crusher, which halts mining production at a cost of anywhere from $1,000 to $5,000 a minute.
4. Asking, "How will this help our employees?" Everyone is motivated by self-interest, so you must gain buy-in by tapping into how the process will make each employee's life better. You can do this in two ways. For this project, we first gathered management and the employees involved and defined short-term vs. long-term benefits. We discussed that improving quality reduces rework in the long term but may require learning new steps or methods in the short term. After facilitated discussions, the employees and supervisors understood this and were prepared for an adjustment period. It was important that we were honest and walked the workers through these steps so they could partner with us to solve these problems.

Second, we personalized the issue by asking if employees enjoy reworking teeth (i.e., by reforging and requenching them), finding storage within limited space, and reducing investment in better machinery (not to mention employee bonuses) due to extensive losses caused by these issues. This type of discussion between management and employees made the problems real and not something they could look past just to get "their" part of the job complete. Employees learned they were responsible for every step in the process as well as the finished product, not just the one stage they oversaw.

5. Review the actual methods used previously—not the "official" documented version but the actual, everyday methods. Gaining trust from the workforce is of paramount importance, and this step in the process shows you why. Initially, management experienced lying due to fear of reprisal (historically, supervisors would treat employees terribly), but after some facilitation, assurances, and honest conversations about the bigger picture related to quality, employees started to share honestly.

If people fear reprisal, they will lie about the numbers or actual methods, and you will not be able to properly interpret the data and make the necessary adjustments. Human interaction and communication is reciprocal, and trust is the basis for open dialogue. Without trust, you have no dialogue, but rather the simple, brute-force power that tends to be inherent in a typical management structure.

Here are two quick ways management decided to improve trust:

a. We invited employees to help solve the problems. Employees often know more about the machine, product, or actual process performed each day than anyone else and generally have great ideas if management will take the time to ask—and listen.

b. I encouraged management to admit mistakes. Employees knew when management made mistakes, and nothing destroys trust quicker than pointing fingers or accusing those who cannot stand up for themselves. Conversely, trust started improving when management took steps to accept responsibility for its mistakes. I coached managers to model the behavior they needed to see in their employees. This created the basis for a "learning organization."

In our example, employees were busy and would often leave teeth in the quench tank while they did other work. As a result, teeth would stay in quench for anywhere from 4 to 30 minutes (the optimal time is 6 to 7 minutes). The control methods used up to this point were cell phones or a stopwatch hanging from a workbench, but the practice was inconsistent at best.

6. Create a concise plan and measure changes. Employees suggested that management purchase and attach a large, 12-in. numbered digital timer and buzzer to the quench tank with a remote control that they could set from the forklift. As employees did other tasks, they could easily monitor the quench-tank timer from a distance. It was a great idea, an inexpensive and easy way to correct the timing issue.

    This improved the process, but then another issue was discovered. It was determined that the liquid used in the tank was not being recycled efficiently enough, and therefore the temperature of the solution was not consistent. This had been suspected and talked about between employees and management, but now management faced the bitter facts and invested in a better pump and recycling method.

7. Follow through consistently. Old habits cannot be stopped; they must be replaced by a new routine or "keystone habit." In other words, the new habit or routine must be recorded over the old habit and positively reinforced consistently for it to become a permanent "keystone" habit. For the first 30 days after the new process started, employees and management monitored the process and results daily, making slight adjustments as needed to hit the target numbers. Successful heat ranges and hardness became consistent, and this helped to naturally reinforce the process and develop confidence in these habits as well as between employees and management.

8. Measure and refine. Be sure to monitor the new process daily, then weekly, and adjust as necessary.

9. Anticipate awkwardness. Until a new process becomes a habit, workers as well as managers will be at risk of reverting to the old habit. I discussed this with the team and reframed mistakes as normal, emphasizing that they should be discussed so everyone could learn and improve. In our example, the department supervisor was trained and coached to see the big picture and choose product quality over sheer quantity as well as to provide employees with encouragement. Also, management and workers discussed the organizational objectives together, so they had buy-in. In this way, everyone came to see and understand the goal, and provided information that led to further reductions in costs and improved bottom-line results.

10. Debrief what worked and what didn't, and refine accordingly. Debriefing about successes and failures is one of the most effective tools a team must leverage organizational learning, and yet it is the least used. People

do not have time to debrief for 10 minutes, but they seem to find time to replicate the mistakes numerous times each year. Management and employees debriefed the process and methods used, which were documented and put into protective plastic sheaths so they could be accessed easily on the shop floor. These documents are not written in stone: The search for better methods should always be encouraged and new processes documented accordingly.

It is management's role to improve the organization's performance and make sure that new and better processes are vetted, adapted, and utilized. Getting buy-in for new steps need not be a challenge if these simple behavioral processes are kept in mind so that employees and management work together throughout the process from inception to implementation.

Challenges such as these can divide a team further, but if coordinated and facilitated properly, they can be used to steer organizations toward success. Because of this challenge, the employees, and management of ABC learned to discuss problems and discover solutions together. In addition, they learned to struggle and work through differences, which helped them work toward a successful and profitable conclusion. These skills are now being used to help ABC address other challenges.

Summary

Organizational skills and behaviors are the way a collective group of people representing a company employs action to demonstrate who they are and what's important to them. The manifestation of these is critical to the success of all organizations and demonstrates a company's willingness to translate thought, theory, and planning into action.

A successful team is more than a group of people working with one another, and it takes focused intent for those who want to be the best of the best. There are five discrete prerequisites for a team that wishes to join this elite class of super professionals:

1. *High commitment.* If one member is not committed, it is best to replace that person. Skills can be taught; commitment cannot.
2. *High levels of trust.* For a group of people to evolve into a team, trust must be the bedrock upon which they build their relationships. It is in

this free-flowing exchange of ideas that genius starts to unfold and one person's idea sparks others.

3. *Desire to achieve as a group.* Once the team has created this dynamic two or three times, it becomes invigorating and self-propelling.

4. *Understanding strengths and weaknesses.* Members make adjustments for each other, and differences become strengths as the team instinctively comes to understand who to rely on given the nature of the problem to be solved.

5. *Dedication to self-development.* It is vital to the success of the team that each member can look within himself or herself and self-correct when necessary.

Morning huddles are designed to be quick, direct, and to the point, just like huddles in football. The idea is to get everyone on the same page, whether that means establishing the goals for the next four to eight hours in a warehouse or on a production line. The morning huddle is also often used to debrief the previous day's events.

Without a doubt, the debrief is one of the most valuable yet least-practiced techniques in the manager's arsenal. Gather the team together into a confined place. Discuss what went well and how the team can repeat those successes. Just focus on repeating the successes, and don't worry about any mistakes.

Evolved executive teams go deeper and discuss people, problems, and solutions. For example, let's say that at the weekly meeting it is decided that a regional office has become complacent, and that the manager and the staff will be given development to improve their performance. There are several issues that would need to be addressed and resolved to accomplish this goal, such as the following:

■ Who will travel to the regional offices and gather information and determine baseline performance?

■ What issues need to be discussed among the executive team (and then with the manager and the staff) to improve the situation?

■ How are these developmental duties to be split between the executive team and the regional management?

■ When will this endeavor begin?

■ What will constitute success?

■ What will be done to follow up and ensure ongoing development?

■ How often should progress be monitored?

Chapter 8

Culture

> Culture is an abstraction, yet the forces that are created in social and organizational situations deriving from culture are powerful. If we don't understand the operation of these forces, we become victim to them. Cultural forces are powerful because they work outside of our awareness. We need to understand them not only because of their power but also because they help to explain many of our puzzling and frustrating experiences in social and organizational life. Most importantly, understanding cultural forces enables us to understand ourselves better.
>
> **Schein 2010**

In recent years, the term "culture" has sprung up everywhere you look. It seems that everyone is trying to find the holy grail of the perfect culture so that they can bottle and sell it. Some believe that there is such a thing as a "right" or "wrong" culture. The implication is that simply by modeling the correct one, your organization will automatically rise to stardom. One client of mine thought that Google's culture was superior because they had a game room, provided massages, and allowed people to bring their pets to work. Because of this belief, he introduced these concepts into his company in hopes they would make his people happy, and success would follow. It didn't; the new features simply added to his overhead. In essence, whether or not a culture is better or worse, effective or not, depends not on the culture alone but on the relationship between the culture and the environment in which it exists.

Culture is often found just below the surface of a group's conscious thoughts, which makes it tough to comprehend and harder to change.

Said another way, culture is to a group what a personality is to an individual. One can see the behavior, but cannot often see the underlying forces that create it. Therefore, just as one's personality guides and constrains behavior, culture guides and constrains the behavior of members of a group through the shared norms of that group. Culture implies that rituals, climate, values, and behaviors tie together into a coherent whole. This pattern is the essence of culture, and such patterning ultimately derives from the human need for our environments to be as sensible and orderly as possible.

To make these rather abstract concepts a bit easier to understand, let me provide examples of what Schein (2010) defines as corporate culture:

- Observed behaviors when people interact. This refers to the language that is used, the customs and traditions that evolve, and the rituals that are employed.
- Group norms. These are the unspoken standards and values that evolve in groups.
- Espoused values. These are expressed principles and values that the group claims to be working toward, such as being recognized as the "low-priced leader" or offering "outstanding customer service."
- Formal philosophy. This represents the broad policies and moral or ethical principles that guide a group's behaviors for customers, employees, and stockholders.
- Rules of the game. These are unwritten mandates about how people need to behave in order to get along in the company or department. These rules are often expressed as "the way we do things around here," which new employees must learn to be accepted by the group.
- Climate. This is the feeling conveyed in a group by the physical layout of the working space, as well as the ways in which members interact with each other, customers, and outsiders.
- Embedded skills. These are the unique capabilities exhibited by group members in accomplishing tasks; they can be thought of as the ability to make certain things, which get passed from generation to generation without being written down.
- Habits of thinking, mental models, and linguistic paradigms. These are shared thoughts that guide the perceptions and language used by members of the group and that are taught to new members.
- Shared meanings. These are developing understandings that are created by group members as they communicate with each other.

- Root metaphors or integrating symbols. These are the ways groups evolve to describe themselves, which is projected into office layouts, buildings, and other material artifacts of the group.
- Structural stability. This works as a stabilizing force after we achieve group identity and is not given up easily. Culture is tough to change because group members value stability, which provides meaning and predictability.
- Depth. As mentioned before, culture is the deepest, often unconscious part of a group and is, therefore, less tangible and visible.
- Breadth. Culture is inescapable and influences all aspects of how a company deals with its primary task, its environments, and its operations. When we speak of culture, we are referring to all of the operations of the organization in question.

In summary, the human mind needs cognitive stability. Anything that disrupts this stability will release anxiety and defensiveness. Culture provides members with a basic sense of identity and defines the values that provide self-esteem. Culture communicates to the group members who they are, how to behave toward one another, and how to feel good about themselves.

> The biggest danger in trying to understand culture is to oversimplify it. It is tempting—and at some level valid—to say that culture is "just the way we do things around here," "the rights and rituals of our company," "the company climate," "the reward system," "our basic values", and so on. These are all manifestations of the culture, but none is the culture at the level where culture matters. A better way to think about culture is to realize that it exists at several "levels," and that we must understand and manage the deeper levels.
>
> **Schein 2010**

The Two Basic Levels of Culture

The levels of culture go from the strategic and highly visible to the tactical and invisible (Schein 2010).

The first level is that of artifacts. This is the easiest level to observe when you walk into an organization. It's what you see, hear, and feel as you walk around. Think about clothing stores, car dealerships, restaurants, food outlets, and hotels. Note your observations and emotional reactions to the architecture, the décor, and the climate, based on how people behave toward you and each other.

You can sense immediately that different companies do things in different ways. At Build.com, which is a Northern California–based Internet company that sells home improvement supplies, people are constantly flowing into and out of meetings with each other. Therefore, the company office structure has very few walls or closed doors. The employees dress informally; there is a feeling of intensity and you get a sense of very fast-paced action. At Davis Engineering, on the other hand, you see people behind closed doors, conversations are hushed, the dress is formal, and you get a sense of careful deliberation and slow, methodical movement. As a client or new employee, you may like or dislike one or the other of these companies, and you may think that's because Build.com and Davis Engineering have different cultures. But you have to be careful. All you know for sure is that they have particular ways of presenting themselves and interacting with each other. You may not know what all of that means, however.

In other words, at the artifact level, culture is very clear and has an immediate emotional impact. Within that reality, however, you don't know why the members of the company are behaving as they do and why each company is created in the way it is. One cannot decipher what is going on just by walking around and observing. The only way to do that is to talk with insiders and ask them questions about the things you observe and feel. This takes you to the next level of culture.

The second basic level of culture is that of espoused values. In other words, the essence of culture is found in the jointly learned values, beliefs, and assumptions that become shared and taken for granted as the company matures. It is imperative that you remember that this expertise resulted from a joint learning process. Originally, they were just in the minds of the founders. They became shared and taken for granted only as the new members of the company realized that the beliefs, values, and assumptions of the founders led to company success and so must be right.

People must realize that culture is stable and difficult to change because it represents the accumulated learning of the group—the ways of thinking, feeling, and perceiving that made the company successful. If asked, people cannot easily tell you about their culture any more than a fish could tell you about the water surrounding it.

Putting It into Practice

Now that I have briefly outlined what culture is, let's examine ways of shifting it from point A to point B. The key is to start small and go slow. Because culture is built on successful outcomes, we must look closely at what is not working and introduce a better method. The successful processes must be duplicated and built upon.

There are several typical stages of a successful cultural change process:

1. Long-term pain or friction between individuals and departments within the company resulting in reduced growth and margins. In my experience, poor business functioning has been plaguing the company for an average of seven years before outside professional help is requested.
2. Reaching out for help to various advisors or consultants. Most organizations I work with have hired advisors who teach the theory behind what successful organizations do to be successful. This type of passive learning doesn't work because it fails to address the changes in behavior necessary to create substantial change in the cultural system. The second type of consultant brought in is often an MBA who specializes in business functions and models, but these typically address superficial symptoms and gloss over the core issues of communication and trust. Yet these very issues are the most important ones in walking members of the system through a cultural shift process. These two methods meet with varying levels of success and failure but very rarely get at the root causes of the failure to successfully shift the culture.
3. Venting. Members of the system about to undertake a cultural shift have lived with fear, anxiety, and despair for an average of seven years. That means they have a lot of pent-up frustration that needs to be vented and released. This is a crucial step or they won't hear anything and won't be able to get past their pain.
4. Honest dialogue around fear, anxiety, and hope. Only after the members have thoroughly vented about being mistreated, taken advantage of, and perhaps even lied to are they in a position to listen and work toward a resolution. This is an important step. Members must be encouraged to vent all of their frustrations until they have depleted their reservoirs of anger and hurt. Once this is complete, then they are ready to listen and consider another way. This leads to sparking a glimmer

of hope; until you reach this point, the team members have not fully exhausted their need to vent.

5. The manager accepts part of the responsibility for the communication breakdown. Once the manager takes the first step toward accepting his or her part in the breakdown, the employee will eventually follow suit.

6. Solution-oriented dialogue. This consists of statements such as
   a. What might change look like?
   b. What is your best guess as to what change might look like?
   c. What might be the first small but significant steps toward this change?
   d. How might our department or company be different in six months if we were to implement these changes?

7. Communication. The exchange of ideas between employees and the manager must be free-flowing and honest, with the manager focusing on listening to what is being conveyed.

8. Trust. Once the employees and the manager have gone through the steps of venting, encouraging honest dialogue, accepting mistakes, introducing solution-oriented dialogue, and engaging in free-flowing communication, trust begins to develop. I say "begins" because it is easy at this stage to move too fast, which will make the employee revert to fear and distrust. Feel your way through this stage, which is another way of saying, stretch yourself and employees without causing stretch marks. Keep in mind that humans can absorb only so much change before they are pushed out too far from their comfort zone, at which point they will inevitably recoil. Therefore, the manager must slowly push employees, then back off and allow the changes to become the new normal. Once people have acclimated, the manager can once again push employees to a new level of functioning.

9. Realigning the hierarchy. Very often the manager of a department has good intentions but that individual's personality isn't strong enough to hold the group together. In these situations, a lower member in the hierarchy typically takes on the unofficial leadership role, and the other employees follow this person instead of the manager. I will call this employee "the manipulator" because that is often what he or she is. This individual has a strong personality and can even be considered a bully. When faced with this issue, it is imperative for management to quickly realign the hierarchy and reestablish the manager as the leader. This is a three-step process:

a. The manager must be assessed to determine if he or she is capable of running the department. The underlying issue may be that the manager isn't intelligent enough and so others are following the smarter employee. Another possibility is that the manager does not have a strong-enough personality and so the bully is given leeway to manipulate the situation. In either case, things must change.

b. If the manager is smart enough, and weakness is the issue, then that person must be taught how to grow a backbone. If the manager is not smart enough, leadership must determine if the person is trainable and coachable. If so, train and coach. If not, then termination is the only option.

c. The bullying employee must also be assessed to determine if he or she is trainable and coachable. Management must face the bully head-on regarding this manipulative behavior. As mentioned in Chapter 5, remember the three-day rule applies. After three days, the bully will either quit, go underground, and then stir the pot while pretending to be part of the team (in which case you must terminate) or undergo a complete turnaround and once again become a functioning member of the team.

10. Debrief. Learn what is working (and repeat it) and find out what is not working (and remove it). As mentioned in Chapter 7, debriefs are pivotal in creating an environment where a topic can be dissected. In this way, things that are working well are encoded into the long-term memory of the group and repeated when similar situations arise. Conversely, while debriefing, if tactics and processes are determined to be of no use, then it is here where the team can decide to remove it from their arsenal.

■ Practice. Successful new behaviors must be instilled through regular use; in this way, the ineffective, old behaviors are extinguished and replaced. As hard as people try and as devoted as they might be to the new processes, they may revert to the old patterns of behavior unless the new systems are practiced with weekly monitoring, feedback, and coaching.

■ Maintenance. Even after three to six months have passed, stress can still cause a team to regress to old familiar habits, so maintenance discussions need to take place periodically.

■ Successful group development patterns. Teams and departments vary, but generally speaking, here are some of the qualities of high-performing groups:

– Members of a successful team will be highly committed to the team and its goals. The members will have created trusting relationships when it comes to the work and functioning of the team. This is not to say that the members will be best friends and go out as a group after work. Some members may never be "friends" in the classic sense, but that's OK as long as there is a professional respect between them. When this occurs, they will trust and even admire one another's work abilities. The team will push and stretch one another because they understand one another's strengths and weaknesses. Most of the members will be excited to be part of such a well-functioning team, and this excitement will manifest itself in many creative and beneficial ways.

– A successful team will be very goal-oriented and will have learned how to work through problems as a unit. When the inevitable challenges and friction between members of the group arise, they will have a high probability of working through it on their own; in fact, they will become a better team because of these challenges. They will often celebrate successes as a unit and share in the limelight. Each member will have evolved due to this process and have learned the skills of constructive self-reflection and change. This will trickle down to the team, so they are adept at making swift midcourse corrections when necessary.

– The manager needs to understand that the team needs to be led through coaching and counseling since training took place earlier in their development. Teams prefer some form of measurement so they can track their progress. Unlike most groups, they want to learn and grow and don't fear constructive criticism, which is why they are a successful team and not just a group of people who must work together. Two-way communication between management and employees is the hallmark of a finely tuned team. And lastly, these types of highly evolved teams often don't require a lot of direction, because they know what the objective is and they work toward it willingly and with enthusiasm.

Steps to Shifting Culture

To shift the culture of an organization, you must start at the center and move out to the larger whole. Remember what I wrote earlier in this book about individuals being a system unto themselves? Think systemically. We start by introducing change within the individual; once the individual has learned how to make changes within themselves, we go out one layer to a small group (Figure 8.1).

Once we are successful in creating change with each member of the team, we can then start bringing members into the team and have them focus on working toward a mutual objective. They will go through the same stages outlined in Chapter 3, so they will need time to adjust and become a unit. However, because they were successful at accomplishing this within themselves, it will be much easier for the manager to use those learning points as references with the team. If you manage a large department, keep the groups to no more than seven people. Once success has been achieved in each team, slowly tie the teams together until the whole department or system is functioning as a unit.

Just as we tied individuals together, now we start tying departments together. Once again, we start by having them work together to outline, assess, and solve a problem. Once the organization is communicating, trusting, and working together, we can start slowly shifting paradigms and challenging previously held beliefs.

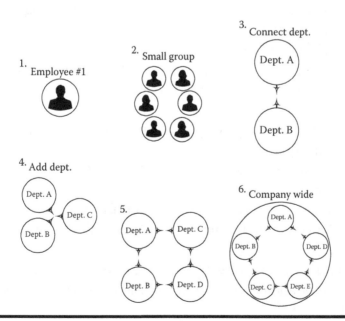

Figure 8.1   Steps to shifting culture.

The Phases of Change: Brandon

New managers often want to do work directly themselves rather than coaching and leading their teams. Take the example of Brandon, mentioned earlier in this book. As you'll recall, Brandon was a conscientious and hardworking employee who was always eager to better himself. He took over the warehouse manager position from his previous manager, who proved unable to adapt to the culture of their rapidly changing and improving organization.

Brandon sustained a high level of drive and demonstrated enthusiasm and a positive attitude when coping with pressures. He worked hard to meet demands at crucial times and showed resilience in the face of challenges and obstacles. Brandon had proven himself to be a valuable employee who could quickly produce a lot of high-quality work by his hands. Although all of this made Brandon a great employee, these very traits stunted his growth as a manager. He was eventually in charge of 40 employees, and his job was to get these people to work in unison. That takes thought and planning.

Originally, Brandon felt that talking about employee development was goofing off; he believed that if he wasn't sweating and straining, he wasn't doing "real work." What Brandon had to learn was that at each level of development, one must learn new skills or they will not progress. Said another way, what made you successful at one stage or level of your career will often sabotage you at the next.

Below are the behaviors and skills that made Brandon a great employee and that told us we had a good candidate for management:

- Took personal ownership (responsibility and accountability) for own work and performance
- Openly acknowledged how things could be improved, and shared solutions for doing so
- Worked autonomously with minimal need for guidance
- Maintained a consistently calm and focused manner, even under pressure
- Worked hard when the pressure was on to meet deadlines
- Volunteered for additional work responsibilities when the department needed it
- Delivered work on time

- Handled multiple priorities at once
- Adapted his approach and showed flexibility when priorities unexpectedly changed

Brandon had to be taught how to develop others and how to shuffle people's responsibilities to create the best dynamics for team production. Brandon and I discussed the various departments and what each needed, which people worked well together, which ones caused friction, and which ones spent too much time gossiping and stirring the pot. As we looked at the whole, we could learn how and where to move people to gain maximum productivity as well as keeping people happy.

During this phase of his development, Brandon learned and then exhibited the following traits:

- Taking responsibility and accountability for the work and performance of others
- Instilling enthusiasm in others to achieve the desired outcome
- Demonstrating a positive attitude even under pressure
- Dismissing the fear of failure

This last point is a most important one. As with most people, Brandon was fearful of making a mistake and looking foolish. He had to be taught that when things don't go as planned, one simply adjusts. Every decision or act cannot be considered as a success or failure; instead, it's preferable to take the view that it's more like an experiment that's planned, executed, assessed, and discussed before adjusting. As time went by, this form of experimentation became a normal process for Brandon, and he quickly lost his fear of "making mistakes." In fact, he began to see that these weren't mistakes at all but rather learning experiences that provided insight into what worked and what didn't. The quicker we could decipher between the two, the faster the goals were achieved.

As Brandon started to make headway, he took personal responsibility and accountability for his work and that of his department. He made timely decisions and committed to a definitive course of action. Brandon accepted when things might have been done better and did not blame other factors. In a nutshell, he

- Helped others to cope with pressures and put those troubles into perspective

- Remained resilient despite obstacles, disappointments, or challenges
- Accepted responsibility for the work in his warehouse and for the way in which results were achieved

The next area Brandon learned about was the always elusive but rarely conquered art of listening. He learned how to ask questions and lead people rather than tell them what to do. He learned how to involve them and listen to them. For example, he learned

- If you tell people what to do, they won't get it.
- If you show people what to do, they may or may not get it.
- If you involve people in the problem and have them actively solve it while you observe and coach, they will understand and get it.

Brandon learned to be excellent at talking with people and not at them. He learned how to ask them for their ideas without the need to take credit, and he learned how to listen and help lead them to better conclusions that were developed by both. This, in turn, created a very trusting and creative dynamic. Other skills and behaviors he developed now included

- Giving practical advice and moral support to employees trying to improve
- Simplifying complex messages from his superiors
- Highlighting and summarizing key points for his team
- "Managing up" to senior executives in a confident and credible way
- Handling problems quickly and efficiently by taking firm and decisive action when a situation required intervention, making tough decisions when necessary, and sticking to appropriate decisions even when they were unpopular

When speaking to senior management, Brandon conveyed complex messages with clarity, presenting a well-structured series of points building toward logical conclusions. This made him stand above his peers and be noticed as a possible future executive in the company (which he ultimately became).

As another sign of his growing stature and ability, Brandon was tasked with monitoring and evaluating multiple and complex projects regularly to check how they were proceeding against deadlines and budget. As he learned how to apply these techniques, Brandon finally learned the value of tackling problems immediately. Problem people, crises, and conflicts between employees no longer bothered him because he had learned the techniques outlined earlier in this book about how best to handle them. He had the tools, which he practiced daily until they were second nature.

The next stage in Brandon's development involved looking into the mirror. Deeply contemplating one's strengths and weaknesses are often the toughest of lessons. Evolved managers learn how to be egoless and self-aware, and to always put the department and company first and one's individual fears and anxieties second.

What gave Brandon the extra edge is that he was good at giving credit to others. Evolved managers give their team the credit when they win and accept the hit when they falter. This creates goodwill and trust since employees on your team will know you put them first in both instances. Nothing builds trust quicker than selfless actions, and nothing ruins a team quicker than a self-serving manager. Evolved managers don't allow their ego to rule them, and they are deeply aware of how they affect others. They continually get coached by those above them so they can evolve and grow to the next level.

Brandon learned that communication is the key differentiator between good managers and great ones. He demonstrated this both when speaking to executives as well as his team, by expressing ideas with tact and clarity. He also provided persuasive and self-assured responses to challenging questions posed by subordinates and superiors alike.

The Two-People Dyad: Tim and Brandon

At Brandon's company was a hardworking, low-level manager by the name of Tim, who had good people skills and an easygoing style. Tim was used to working with guys in the receiving department of the warehouse, and as a small-knit group, they were very successful. But Tim needed to learn how to create the same winning dynamic with 40 employees over five departments occupying 15,000 square feet, not just with five people in a 50-foot by 50-foot corner.

I coached Brandon to develop Tim in the same way I trained Brandon. In this case, Brandon spoke to Tim while I sat and supported Brandon. They began with a discussion of each other's strengths and weaknesses, before laying out a weekly plan with specific goals. These were warehouse goals, mostly, but also included some activities in which Tim was to apply more of his leadership skills and fewer of his hands-on abilities. His duties started shifting from being a worker 100% of the time to 70% worker and 30% assistant manager. Gradually this number kept moving toward the manager side of the equation until Tim could handle the entire warehouse by himself. This allowed Brandon to tackle other challenges, including taking over the management duties of other departments.

Tim had been promoted from the receiving department, so it was running pretty smoothly at that time. Tim and his team knew how to communicate and work as a unit. But because Tim was increasingly stepping out of that position, we had to backfill the lead role. We had a great person who Tim had been training in mind for the position, and he stepped in nicely.

As this process continued, the stocking and picking function was completed by the same crew, as were packing and shipping. We could make these changes with little disruption because we could shepherd subdepartments of 7 to 12 people through the development process outlined earlier. The team-building effort within the warehouse helped create a synergy between departments and helped people see how each team must work as a unit.

Aligning the Warehouse, Customer Service Department, and Marketing

I went through the same process seen above with the customer service department. Once both departments were functioning effectively with trust, communication, and joint problem-solving, it was time to join them together. Leif, the customer service manager, worked closely with Brandon and I as cofacilitators in establishing a joint dialogue between the warehouse and customer service.

Working together, these departments helped internal customers, including other teams within the organization, see opportunities even when faced with obstacles and challenges. They negotiated effectively by identifying common ground and potential solutions that were of mutual benefit. They coordinated input from different subteams to deliver cross-department projects. Most of all, they challenged each other to continuously raise their standards and performance.

We had started this process of cultural shifting with the warehouse because the 24-hour-a-day, 7-days-a-week shipping cycle that Amazon had established had become the industry standard, expected from customers regardless of how big or small that customer's chosen vendor might be.

With the customer journey as the focus, we next wanted to get as close to that customer as possible, and the customer service reps are the ones who touch the customer more often than anyone else. Also, they are in a great position to share information and gather information from the customer.

Finally, we added marketing because of the close relationship marketing needs to have with the customer; after all, marketing professionals are always hungry for information about how well their products are received by customers, as well as suggestions about how to package products and offerings for maximum success. Customer service and marketing needed to work closely together to gather and interpret customer data to ensure ongoing organizational success.

Summary

Culture is often below the surface of our conscious thought and therefore tough to comprehend and harder to change. Said another way, culture is to a group what a personality is to a person. One can see the behavior, but cannot often see the underlying forces that create that behavior. Therefore, just as one's personality guides and constrains behavior, culture guides and constrains the behavior of members within a group through the shared norms of that group.

When people interact, you can observe the language they use, the customs and traditions that evolve, and the rituals that they employ. The unwritten rules for getting along in the company or department, also known as "the way we do things around here," are critically important pieces of information that a new employee must learn to function and be accepted into the group. These include shared meanings, root metaphors, structural stability, and the breadth and depth of the cultural imperatives. Such patterning ultimately derives from the human need to make our environments as sensible and orderly as possible.

In summation, the human mind needs cognitive stability. Thus, anything that disrupts this stability will release anxiety and defensiveness. Culture provides members with a basic sense of identity and defines the values that provide self-esteem. Culture communicates to the group members who they are, how to behave toward one another, and how to feel good about themselves.

Conclusion

Victor Frankl's ground breaking research showed both the best and worst that can come from human interaction. The good news is that people are inherently good. From the new energetic and perhaps naïve employee to the grizzled old-timer and everyone in between, people want something to live for, something to believe in, even something to work toward. It's the job of the evolved manager to paint this picture and back it up with trust and clear two-way communication so that everyone involved can function to the level of the image they have within themselves. For the most part, people want the company they work in to function better.

We all want to be part of a winning team and associate ourselves with others who want the same. More good news is that, as Carol Dweck pointed out in Chapter 5, people's thoughts are malleable, which means they can be shifted from a fixed mindset to a growth mindset if certain guidelines are followed and principles held to. Furthermore, the research of Charles Duhigg and Nathan Azrin shared that once thought can be redirected, then behaviors can quickly follow if consistent behavior modification plans can be strategically employed. But it starts with a good plan and action. One must pull the trigger and execute.

Starting from day one, employees need direction from their managers and when managers guide new and even long-term employees, results can be achieved through consistent effort. This effort can be more finely tuned when the MED Review is leveraged so that the manager and the employee are working in unison. These principles and skills can be leveraged further to include department development through the aid of general systems theory. What a manager can achieve with an individual, he or she can achieve with his or her team. The timing might be different and a bit slower, but the concepts are the same. With time, consistent effort, and a bit more training, one can start to shift the cultural dynamics that are working behind the scenes and under the surface. All in all, every person reading this material can achieve their improvement plans if they simply study this material and apply it. Yes, it is scary to step out of one's comfort zone and apply new techniques to old problems, but what choice do you have? If you have tried other methods and they didn't work for you, then follow the recipe outlined in this book and stretch yourself and those around you. It doesn't matter where you start, but you must start to create change. Furthermore, it's natural to be a bit scared, and it's also natural to step through that fear into the unknown; and when done consistently, the unknown becomes known and before you know it, you are transforming not only yourself but also those around you and as you transform those around you, your career will transform. But it takes one bold step and then another and then another. Here is the secret recipe: Study, walk into the unknown, act, refine, and repeat; study, walk into the unknown, act, refine, and repeat; study, walk into the unknown, act, refine, and repeat.

Appendix

Part One: Self-Development Inquiry

Part Two of the Manager and Employee Development Review Process

1. Take an objective look at your working, management, or leadership style and skills during the past 6–12 months. **Part One:** Please list 2–3 strengths and/or personal characteristics that have helped you excel or be productive as an employee, manager, or leader. **Part Two:** Please list 2–3 limitations that continue to impede your progress as an effective employee, manager, or leader.
2. Please outline 3–5 areas as an employee, manager, or leader where you would like additional training, coaching, and supportive Professional Development. How might these improved skills, business insights, and industry knowledge improve the customer experience? Improve your department and/or company? And advance your personal and professional value as an employee, manager, or leader?

Manager and Employee Development Review Employee

Name: _____ **Date:** _____

Department: _____ **Title:** _____ **Position:** _____

Direct Supervisor: _____ **Title:** _____

Definitions of Performance Ratings:

A—Excellent—Often exceeds all requirements of position. (Suggested development program outlined for additional responsibilities and possible advancement.)

B—Very Capable—Performs above average in position. (Suggested written coaching and development program outlined with regular follow-up in order to become an "A" player.)

C—Satisfactory—Occasionally meets requirements of the position. (Written training, coaching, and perhaps counseling required to help this employee improve. Improvement program must be undertaken with follow-up reviews every month during the next six months.)

D to F—Unsatisfactory—Fails to meet position requirements. (A last ditch effort must be made to transfer to a position better suited to their skills, or a decision must be made to either Train, Coach, Counsel, or Terminate.)

Category	*Rating*
1. **Volume of Work:** Maintains a steady and acceptable level of work	_____
a. Increases pace, if needed, so that deadlines can be met	_____
b. Organizes work in order to obtain high productivity	_____
Supporting example: _____	
2. **Quality of Work:** Maintains acceptable standards of workmanship	_____
a. Completes work thoroughly without requiring constant correction	_____
Supporting example: _____	
3. **Job Knowledge:** Understands job procedures, equipment, methods, responsibilities, and scope of work	_____
a. Understands the operation (and limitations) of work	_____
b. Keeps informed, makes use of proper standards and procedures	_____
Supporting example: _____	

4. **Commitment to Job:** Demonstrates a consistent, dependable work effort and positive work attitude   _____

   a. Is flexible; adapts easily to changes in work assignments   _____

   b. Is eager to take on additional responsibilities   _____

   Supporting example: _____

5. **Attendance and Punctuality:** Uses company time properly   _____

   a. Arrives and leaves at proper time, uses breaks appropriately   _____

   b. Gives proper advance notice in case of absence   _____

   Supporting example: _____

6. **Safety and Maintenance:** Ensures safety of self and others through proper use and care of equipment/work site   _____

   a. Handles and operates equipment in a careful manner   _____

   b. Stores and maintains equipment properly and communicates maintenance issues to proper supervisor according to protocol   _____

   Supporting example: _____

7. **Communicates Information:** Communicates ideas and information in a clear, concise, and timely manner   _____

   a. Provides complete, reliable, and prompt information to supervisor and coworkers   _____

   b. Keeps accurate records of completed work and appropriate documents/work orders   _____

   Supporting example: _____

8. **Cooperation:** Works with others to do a good job for the day and week   _____

   a. Functions well as a team member, gets along with fellow employees   _____

   b. Follows instruction; accepts work assignments willingly   _____

   Supporting example: _____

Joint Development Goals

1. _____
2. _____
3. _____

Purpose: How will this activity improve the department, customer, or production, i.e., quality improvement, quantity improvement, target behavior expected, etc.

1. _____
2. _____
3. _____

Please outline Employee Responsibilities, i.e., methods and actions:

Please outline Supervisor Responsibility, i.e., methods and actions:

Please list <u>expected</u> outcome. Be precise:

Please list <u>actual</u> outcome and date for measurement evaluation, i.e., 30, 60, 90 days:

Employee signature: _____ Date: _____

Supervisor signature: _____ Date: _____

Overall comments from Supervisor:

Employee Remarks:

MED Review Leader/Manager

Name: _____ **Date:** _____

Definitions of Performance Ratings:

A—Excellent—Often exceeds all requirements of position. (Suggested development program outlined for additional responsibilities and possible advancement.)

B—Very Capable—Performs above average in position. (Suggested written coaching and development program outlined with regular follow-up in order to become an "A" player.)

C—Satisfactory—Occasionally meets requirements of the position but is not considered leader or management material unless significant improvements can be made. (Written training, coaching, and perhaps counseling required to help this person improve or failure will result. Weekly and monthly follow-up reviews are mandatory over the next six months.)

D to F—Unsatisfactory—Fails to meet position requirements. (A last ditch effort/decision must be made to transfer or Train, Coach, Counsel, or Terminate. Extremely low probability of success.)

Category	*Rating*
1. **Leadership:** Industry, Organizational, and/or Department visionary. Inspires trust and motivates people	_____
a. Takes charge of people and events: assumes leadership in a positive way	_____
b. Develops future leaders and delegates effectively	_____
2. **Management:** Provides specific direction, follows up, positively develops people, keeps people on task	_____
a. Provides clear, objective, and timely feedback	_____
b. Ensures employees are trained and developed in all aspects of the job	_____
3. **Project Management:** Skilled in planning, logistics, and completing projects on time	_____
a. Exhibits good pre-planning skills and follow-through	_____
b. Breaks large projects down into manageable phases or stages with established measurable goals	_____

4. **Time Management and Organization Skills:**   _____

  a. Manages time efficiently and is able to juggle changing priorities effectively   _____

  b. Exhibits exceptional organization skills   _____

5. **Communication/Interpersonal Skills:** Positive attitude, listens for understanding, relays messages clearly   _____

  a. Holds well-organized and effective meetings   _____

  b. Participates actively in meetings; makes meaningful contributions   _____

6. **Collaboration/Team Player:** Sacrifices personal goals for team success and/or organizational objectives   _____

  a. Motivates others; creates enthusiasm for team effort   _____

  b. Sets a positive example for the department; a model of what to do and how to do it   _____

7. **Professionalism:** Punctual, Responsible, and Accountable   _____

  a. Takes responsibility for his/her own training and development   _____

8. **Problem Solving and Decision Making:**   _____

  a. Observes early signs of changing conditions and offers creative and/or effective solutions   _____

  b. Makes firm decisions (yes/no, not maybe) and follows through to ensure appropriate actions have been taken   _____

9. **Organizational Customer Service:** Inter/intradepartmental customer service   _____

  a. Takes initiative to enquire about internal customer needs and opinions   _____

  b. Encourages, facilitates, and develops inter/intradepartment cooperation   _____

Joint Development Goals

4. _____
5. _____
6. _____

Purpose: How will this activity improve the department, customer, or production, i.e., quality improvement, quantity improvement, target behavior expected, etc.

4. _____
5. _____
6. _____

Please outline Employee Responsibilities, i.e., methods and actions:

Please outline Supervisor Responsibility, i.e., methods and actions:

Please list <u>expected</u> outcome. Be precise:

Please list <u>actual</u> outcome and date for measurement evaluation, i.e., 30, 60, 90 days:

Employee signature: _____ Date: _____

Supervisor signature: _____ Date: _____

Overall comments from Supervisor:

Employee Remarks:

References

Appelbaum, Steven H., Michael Bregman, and Peter Moroz. 1998. "Fear as a Strategy: Effects and Impacts Within the Organization." *Journal of European Industrial Training* 22 (3), 113–127.

Bandura, Albert. 2009. "Handbook of principles of organization behavior." In *Cultivate Self-efficacy for Personal and Organizational Effectiveness*, by Albert Bandura, pp. 179–200. New York: Wiley.

Barry, Lisa, Stacia Garr, and Andy Liakopoulos. 2014. "Performance Management is Broken Replace 'Rank and Yank' with Coaching and Development." Accessed October 1, 2016. https://dupress.deloitte.com/dup-us-en/focus/human-capital -trends/2014/hc-trends-2014-performance-management.html

Bowen, Murray. https://www.thebowencenter.org/theory/eight-concepts /triangles/ March 2016. Concept originally developed and introduced in 1971.

Broad, William. 2004. "Libya's Crude Bomb Design Eases Western Experts' Fear." *The New York Times*, February 9: A7.

Business Strategy. 2012. To Realise Workforce Potential: Manage with a Growth Mindset. October 3. Accessed October 1, 2016. https://www.businessthink .unsw.edu.au/Pages/To-Realise-Workforce-Potential–Manage-with-a-Growth -Mindset.aspx

Cherry, Kendra. 2016. "Motivation: Psychological Factors That Guide Behavior." Accessed September 30, 2016. https://www.verywell.com/what-is-motivation-2795378

Clark, Don. 2009. Visual, Auditory, and Kinesthetic Learning Styles (VAK). Accessed October 1, 2016. http://www.nwlink.com/~donclark/hrd/styles/vakt.html

Dawn, Melissa. 2014. "6 Eye-Opening Employee Engagement Statistics." Accessed October 1, 2016. http://www.talentculture.com/6-eye-opening-employee -engagement-statistics/

DeGouveia, CM. 2005. "Towards a Typology of Gossip in the Workplace." *SA Journal of Human Resource Management* 3 (2), 56–68.

Duhigg, Charles. 2012. *The Power of Habit*. New York: Random House.

Dweck, Carol S. 2008. *Mindset: The New Pschology of Success*. New York: Ballantine Books.

Frankl, Victor E. 2006. *Man's Search for Meaning*. Boston: Beacon Press.

Galinsky, Adam. 2008. "Power Reduces the Press of the Situation: Implications for Creativity, Conformity, and Dissonance." *American Psychological Association* 95 (6), 1450–1466.

Glei, Jocelyn K. n.d. "Talent Isn't Fixed and Other Mindsets That Lead to Greatness When We Welcome the Creative Struggle We're More Likely to Succeed." Accessed October 1, 2016. http://99u.com/articles/14379 /talent-isnt-fixed-and-other-mindsets-that-lead-to-greatness

Graves, Kelly. 2015. "Employee Evaluations Are a Waste of Time and Money." Accessed October 1, 2016. http://www.qualitydigest.com/inside/management -column/102615-employee-evaluations-are-waste-time-and-money.html

Graves, Kelly. 2016a. "Seven Steps to Better Performance." Accessed October 1, 2016. http://www.qualitydigest.com/inside/management-column/090215-seven -steps-better-performance.html

Graves, Kelly. 2016b. "'Us' vs. 'Them' Inc." March 22. Accessed September 30, 2016. http://www.qualitydigest.com/inside/management-column/032216-us-vs-them -inc.html#

Heslin, Peter A. 2005. "The Effects of Implicit Person Theory on Performance Appraisals." *Journal of Applied Psychology*, 842–856.

Heslin, Peter A. 2006. "Keen to Help? Managers Implicit Person Theories and Their Subsequent Employee Coaching." *Personnel Psychology*, Winter.

HR Pros of the HR Support Center. 2014. "The Top 10 Performance Review Biases." Accessed October 1, 2016. https://www.paycor.com/resource-center /the-top-10-performance-review-biases

Juniata. 2011. APA Performance Evaluations. Accessed September 30, 2016. http:// legacy.juniata.edu/services/hresources/documents/WhitePaperPerformanceReview Evaluations.pdf

Kets de Vries, Manfred F.R. 2009. "The Shadow Side of Leadership." *Human Capital Review and Etdonline*, South Africa.

Kim, Ben. 2012. Meaning. Accessed September 30, 2016. http://drbenkim.com /meaning

Knowledge@Wharton. 2011. Should Performance Reviews Be Fired? April 27. Accessed October 1, 2016. http://knowledge.wharton.upenn.edu/article /should-performance-reviews-be-fired/

Konnikova, Maria. 2015. "The Real Lesson of the Stanford prison Experiment." *The New Yorker.com*, June 15.

Mcleod, Saul A. 2016. Zimbardo—Stanford Prison Experiment. http://www.simply psychology.org/zimbardo.html

Merzenich, Michael. 2009. *Growing evidence of brain plasticity*. Performed by Michael Merzenich. TED Talks.

Mosley, Eric. 2012. Crowdsource Your Performance Reviews. June 15. Accessed October 1, 2016. https://hbr.org/2012/06/crowdsource-your-performance-r

Neal, David. 1996. "Habits: A Repeat Performance." *Duke University Study* Volume 15 #4.

Ormrod, Jeanne E. 2006. *Educational Psychology: Developing Learners*. Upper Saddle River: Pearson/Merril Prentice Hall.

Ormrod, Jeanne E. 1999. *Human Learning (3rd ed)*. Upper Saddle River, NJ: Prentice Hall.

Pfeffer, Jeffrey. 1999. "The Knowing-Doing Gap." Stanford Graduate School of Business. November 1. Accessed September 30, 2016. https://www.gsb .stanford.edu/insights/knowing-doing-gap

Roberts, Gary and Michael Pregitzer. 2007. "Why Employees Dislike Performance Appraisals." Accessed October 1, 2016. https://www.regent.edu/acad/global /publications/rgbr/vol1iss1/performance_appraisals.shtml

Rock, David. 2014. "Kill Your Performance Ratings." August 8. Accessed September 30, 2016. http://www.strategy-business.com/article/00275?gko=c442b

Ryan, Richard M. and Edward L. Deci. 2000. "Self-determination Theory and the Facilitation of Intrinsic Motivation, Social Development, and Well-being." *American Psychology* 55 (1), 68–78.

Schein, Edgar. 2010. *Organizational Culture and Leadership*. San Francisco: Jossey-Bass.

Selden, Sally. 2013. www.shrm.org. Accessed October 1, 2016. http://www.shrm .org/qualityoftheirperformanceappraisalsystems

Seltzer, Leon F. 2008. "What Your Anger May Be Hiding." July 11. Accessed September 30, 2016. https://www.psychologytoday.com/blog/evolution-the-self /200807/what-your-anger-may-be-hiding

Suu Kyi, Aung San. 1996. *Freedom from Fear*, Penguin books.

University of Pennsylvania. 2009. "Visual Learners Convert Words To Pictures In The Brain And Vice Versa, Says Psychology Study." ScienceDaily. Accessed January 24, 2017. www.sciencedaily.com/releases/2009/03/090325091834.htm

Vaden, Chris. 2004. "Punishment: Benefits, Risks, and Alternatives in a Business Setting." Accessed September 30, 2016. http://digitalcommons.liberty.edu/cgi /viewcontent.cgi?article=1201&context=honors

VanBogaert, Dan. n.d. "New Legal Battlegrounds for Performance Evaluations." Accessed October 1, 2016. http://myweb.lmu.edu/dbogaert/newlegalbattleground spedvb.pdf

Weiss, Alan. 2000. *The Unofficial Guide to Power Managing*. IDG Books pages 80–84.

Wendy. 2013. "7 Reasons Why I Hate Performance Appraisals." July 9. Accessed September 30, 2016. https://7geese.com/7-reasons-why-i-hate-performance -appraisals/

Williams, Ray. 2014. "Why Performance Appraisals Don't Improve Performance." November 7. Accessed October 1, 2016. https://www.psychologytoday.com/blog /wired-success/201402/why-performance-appraisals-dont-improve-performance

Wolfe, Catherine. 2004. *2004 U.S. Master Human Resource Guide*. Chicago, IL: CCH, Inc.

Index